NONPROFIT STARTUP GUIDE

SERVE YOUR COMMUNITY QUICKLY WITH CONFIDENCE AND REDUCED STRESS

LYNN CORDOVA

CONTENTS

INTRODUCTION

Every good act is charity. A man's true wealth here-after is the good that he does in this world to his fellows.

— MOLIERE

Reported statistics show that in the United States alone, there are about 1.8 million nonprofit organizations (Reasonover, 2021). The global projection of nonprofit and nongovernmental organizations is above 10 million (Reasonover, 2021). However, although such a considerable number of nonprofit organizations have already been established, there is a high chance that they are outnumbered by the people who need assistance. If you are passionate about giving back to the community by setting up a nonprofit organization, there is always a gap that you can fill.

Even if you have a burning urge and desire to start a nonprofit organization, knowledge of how to begin and complete the process is crucial. If you are one of those people who is hesitant to start because you did not have the answers to the "how," "what," "when," "who," and "what" questions yet, then this book is for you. You might have kickstarted the process of starting the organization but gave up somewhere along the way because it all seemed so complicated and overwhelming. Again, if this relates to you, the information included here will help get you back on track.

Could you be one of those people who are keen to give back to the community, but you prefer founding a charitable organization instead of taking advantage of ones that already exist? Perhaps, similar existing nonprofit organizations may not exactly fill the need you see in your community. However, with this book in your hands, rest assured that you will gain the ability and confidence to complete the whole process on your own in a less time-consuming manner. This book is a route to fulfilling the desire to be like those nonprofit organization owners whom you look up to, and you will be grateful to yourself for being brave enough to do it on your own.

This book presents information on the various classifications of nonprofit corporations and the pros and cons of running a nonprofit organization. You will also be furnished with tips on creating a strategic plan, developing a budget, selecting a board, setting up a strong online presence, and creating the necessary documentation to apply for tax exemption. There is no prescribed waiting period before you can start applying the takeaways from this book. You can begin the implementation process immediately and take the first step on your journey to serve your community!

WHY I WROTE THIS BOOK

I have always had the desire to start my own equine-assisted learning nonprofit. An avid horseback rider, I knew the power of healing that horses could provide. My experience in the education field also led me to realize the various ways children learn. Combining these two concepts led me to the idea of helping children through equine involvement. To accomplish this, I started volunteering at a similar facility and took note of best practices. The organization I volunteered with was highly successful, but over a thirty-minute drive from my community. I considered approaching them to develop a partnership whereby I could operate as a second location, but honestly, I did not know how this would work. I realize now I could have asked them to be a fiscal sponsor, which we will discuss in Chapter 7. I ultimately decided to start my own nonprofit because I felt my community had a need that would be better served by an equine-assisted learning facility that was more readily accessible. I also wanted to focus on a different population of clients.

However, when I started researching how to legally form my own nonprofit, I was frustrated by a lack of resources. Yes, the information is out there, but as a single mom of three boys with a full-time job, I struggled to find time to consolidate all the information found in various places. The process took longer for me than it should have because there was not a clear resource that explained the order in which I was supposed to have the required items, as well as a full description of the documents that were necessary to satisfy the legal requirements. It was also frustrating to discover phrasings required for Form 1023, the tax-exempt application in the United States, which I luckily discovered before submitting paperwork with my state filing.

Helping you start a nonprofit matters deeply to me because I feel strongly that loving others by serving them is the key to happiness. Not only does it impact the lives of those you serve, but it also changes your own perspective regarding life in general. Some individuals simply do not have enough financial resources to hire professionals to assist them in the various steps required to start their nonprofit organizations. Therefore, doing it on their own is the only cost-effective option possible. The process to enable you to begin serving should not be cost- or time-prohibitive, nor should it be so overwhelmingly complex that it discourages you from getting started. I sincerely desire that this book helps you ignite your dream of starting and running a nonprofit organization, thereby bringing it to life.

1

DETERMINING NONPROFIT CLASSIFICATION

Most likely, you are reading this book because you have decided to form a nonprofit to address a need in your community. Some of you may be well-versed in business and others may not know where to start. This chapter will provide a high-level overview of basic business structures so that you can confidently decide if the nonprofit route is right for your specific situation. After reading this chapter, you will understand the various options available for structuring your nonprofit organization in five countries: Australia, Canada, Ireland, the United Kingdom, and the United States.

BUSINESS TYPES

A corporation is an entity that could be created by a group of people or an individual but is legally regarded and treated as one individual. Many of the rights and expectations that individuals have also apply to corporations. For example, both can hire employees, pay taxes, borrow and lend money, and face legal repercussions if they go against the law.

Most of the large businesses you know are **for-profit corporations,** such as Coca-Cola Co and Microsoft Corp. For-profit organizations are set up to create revenue for the benefit of the owners and other shareholders and investors, if any. To make profits, these organizations offer services or goods that customers can pay for.

A **nonprofit corporation** operates for a collective social or public benefit, such as national charities, churches, universities, and hospitals. Examples range from Relief International, a development and humanitarian nonprofit alliance resulting from the merger of four organizations and employing over 5,000 people, to Pink Ribbon Moms, a small group of fewer than ten people supporting moms who have lost a daughter to breast cancer.

For-profit and nonprofit corporations share similarities, such as electing a board of directors, conducting annual meetings, and adopting bylaws.

In the United States, a **limited liability company** (LLC) is another type of legal entity that can be formed to own and operate a business. This structure combines the features of a corporation and a partnership. The main advantage for the business is that the profits and taxes required on the profits are the responsibility of the owners of the LLC rather than the company itself.

It is important to note that the nomenclature describing how an organization is formed may vary by jurisdiction, which we will explain in more detail later. However, all the descriptions and definitions still have one thing in common—limited liability. The term "limited liability" describes a scenario where shareholders (for a corporation), owners/members (for a limited liability company), or founders (for a nonprofit) are not, in their capacity as individuals, responsible for liability (for example, debts) that the company may incur. This is the primary advantage of incorporating your nonprofit venture.

FIVE-STEP TEST

The five-step test can help you determine whether you should set up your organization as a nonprofit or for-profit entity. Review the questions posed in each section and honestly answer based on your business idea. You can still help others with a for-profit entity - think of companies like Toms that sell a pair of shoes and give away a pair of shoes.

Primary Purpose and Mission

Every organization has a primary purpose, but does yours conform to the requirements of the traditional nonprofit classification? You need to assess if your organization's mission is oriented toward religious, charitable, or educational goals. Basically, you are looking at whether you look forward to benefiting from the organization's proceeds or if it is solely for public benefit.

Unrelated Business Income (UBI)

Are you, by any chance, considering collecting business income that is unrelated to the nonprofit mission that you envision? In small amounts, this practice could bring in additional income that helps to achieve the mission; however, if a nonprofit collects too much unrelated business income, it could be at risk of losing its tax-exempt status and owing back taxes. Therefore, asking yourself now if you foresee this as an issue is essential. Let's take a school as an example. Tuition payments are related to its exempt purpose, as it is important for the entity's functioning. However, suppose the school decides to set up a retail shop to sell clothes which ends up providing a majority of the school's income. In that case, the retail income may become an issue, even if the proceeds contribute to running the organization. This is because selling clothes is completely unrelated to the normal business that the school carries out on a daily basis (NP, 2011).

Funding Methods

Generally, funding sources for nonprofit organizations include donations and grants. They are allowed to source funds from both private and public grants. Contrastingly, for-profit organizations may apply for small business loans and accommodate shareholder investors who aim to earn profits. Nonprofit organizations are prohibited from any acts where owners financially benefit from the organization. Similarly, it cannot distribute profits to investors. Therefore, you can use funding strategies to determine whether you would rather run your organization as a nonprofit or for-profit.

Nonprofit companies formed for public benefit are associated with tax-exempt status, meaning individuals can donate funds and receive a tax-deductible receipt. The nonprofit organization does not have to pay taxes on this income. Purchases may also be sales tax-free in some states or regions. However, if your organization has employees, you are still expected to pay state and federal payroll taxes.

Control of the Organization

Nonprofit organizations are governed by a board of directors, who are also responsible for making relevant decisions concerning the entity's operations. In a for-profit corporation, the founder can maintain control over the majority of shares and vote those shares according to their personal preferences. You cannot exercise individual control in a nonprofit organization. Based on the laws, the company is expected to have a board of directors who have decision-making powers.

Personal Payouts

How do you intend to be paid? Most nonprofits allow for a reasonable salary for Executive Directors and other employees while the nonprofit is up and running. However, there is no payout to a founder or staff members upon the dissolution of a nonprofit. Instead, any remaining funds are paid out to another nonprofit.

However, for-profit corporations provide dividends to their shareholders.

Any financial proceeds that are given to or made by a nonprofit organization are not used for the employees' personal benefit. Rather, they are invested in advancing the mission and purpose of the organization. This is why all financial records are public so that donors and other relevant people may see if funds are being used according to the stipulated purpose.

DIFFERENT TYPES OF PUBLIC BENEFIT ORGANIZATIONS

In this section, we assume you have already completed a basic determination of for-profit versus nonprofit. We also extrapolate that you now want to know how exactly to structure your nonprofit. Therefore, this section will review different types of public benefit organizations.

Nonprofit Organization

Let's discuss the different types of nonprofit organizations based in various countries.

Ireland

In Ireland, nonprofit organizations are legally structured into three forms: an unincorporated association, a trust, or a company limited by guarantee (CLG). We will describe these legal structures in more detail.

An Unincorporated Association

Forming an unincorporated association is based on written or oral consent by the individuals involved, which explains why it is relatively easy to create. It is governed by a set of rules interpreted based on contract law. Unincorporated associations are not recognized as legal persons, so they cannot stand alone as far as the law is concerned. In fact, the members of the unincorporated association shoulder the responsibility for the organization's debts.

Many groups start as unincorporated associations and later transition to incorporated status as they grow, expand activities, and employ people. As the operations and nature of the organization become more complex, the members may see the need to be protected from being personally liable for its debts.

A Trust

The main characteristic of trusts is that an individual or group of people are given the authority to hold property or funds for others. The authority these people have is in the form of a governing instrument called the "deed of trust." The main issues addressed by the deed of trust are the appointment and authority of trustees, their removal, and the trust's aims and objectives.

A common attribute between trusts and unincorporated associations is that both are not regarded as legal persons. Therefore, the members are liable for any debts that may be associated with the organization. However, it is feasible for a trust to be converted into a corporate body.

A Company Limited by Guarantee (CLG)

You can think of a CLG as an alternative form of a corporation. Nonprofit organizations that need to attain a legal personality can apply for CLGs. Members of CLGs are not shareholders; they are guarantors who contribute certain amounts of money to keep the organization going. No profits are distributed to the organization's members, which is one of the reasons why the association qualifies for charitable tax exemption.

Based on the Companies Act 2014, you might come across the term "Designated Activity Company" (DAC). The DAC is similar to the CLG in that both require a memorandum of association to stipulate their purpose. However, a DAC has share capital, which is unlike the CLG. Therefore, organizations requiring tax exemption should stick to the CLG format.

United States

Nonprofit organizations at the federal level in the United States are characterized by different designations, even though all are generally classified as 501 (c) organizations. Various requirements and expectations are associated with different 501 (c) nonprofit organization designations. For a summary of each type, see Appendix A.

The largest category of nonprofits in the United States are 501(c)(3) nonprofits, which are divided into two segments.

- Public charities - receive financial support from various sources such as individuals, foundations, and government entities and/or from activities related to the tax-exempt purpose. Some types of organizations like churches, schools, and hospitals automatically qualify as public charities.
- Private foundations - may support similar causes as public charities, but are funded by individuals or a small group of donors and use their money to provide grants to other organizations. There are strict operating limitations and taxes unique to private foundations to discourage wealthy individuals

and families from using the private foundation designation to avoid taxes.

Chapter 7 will review the details for applying for tax-exempt status for 501 (c)(3) organizations that are operating as public charities only. Still, every chapter contains helpful information for all types of 501 (c) organizations (for example, strategic planning, budgeting, and creating an online presence).

Not-For-Profit

Do "nonprofit" and "not-for-profit" organizations refer to the same thing? Certainly not, but many people confuse these two phrases. Find out the difference in this section.

United States

A not-for-profit organization (NFPO) is similar to a nonprofit organization in that both do not generate profits for the owners. All the money that the NFPO makes or receives is used to run the organization to fulfill its purpose. The difference between nonprofits and NFPOs is that the latter is not expected to work toward public benefit.

Think of a strength-training club as a good example of an NFPO. Any money donated to such an organization is used for the benefit of the club members, not the public. NFPOs can apply to the IRS only for sales and property taxes exemption. This is why if an individual donates money to an NFPO, it will not be deducted from their tax return.

The other main differences between nonprofits and NFPOs are as follows:

- Nonprofit organizations can operate as separate legal entities while NFPOs cannot.
- Nonprofit organizations can operate the same way as any regular business and earn profits used to pursue their mission. However, this is different for NFPOs, which are usually regarded as recreational organizations.
- Nonprofit organizations can employ people whom they pay for their services. In NFPOs, volunteers run the show.

United Kingdom

In the United Kingdom, NFPOs exist in five forms, which are:

- companies limited by guarantee (CLG)
- trusts
- unincorporated associations
- charitable incorporated organizations

- registered societies

All these types of NFPOs qualify to operate as charities. This, in turn, means that they can apply for tax exemption as long as they meet the stipulated requirements.

Australia

In Australia, NFPOs are categorized into two types: charities and other NFPOs. The term "charity," in legal terms, does not simply refer to an organization that offers some form of assistance to the community. Apart from not operating for profits, organizations that are categorized as charities also have the following attributes:

- Their activities enhance religion or education.
- They assist people who are disadvantaged.
- Their operations benefit the community in one way or another.

Based on these characteristics, animal care societies, disability service organizations, elderly care homes, and environmental protection groups are all examples of charities. In addition, arts or cultural groups and some religious groups also fall under this category of NFPOs.

Other examples of NFPOs in Australia worth mentioning are community service organizations, social societies, recreational clubs, and business and professional associations. These organizations operate to the benefit of either their members or the communities that they serve.

Registered Charity

Canada

In Canada, charitable organizations are described as such, as well as public or private foundations founded and operating within the country. The mandate of these organizations is to carry out charitable activities using their resources. Their purpose falls within the boundaries of the following classifications:

- religion advancement
- education advancement
- poverty relief
- other mandates that are beneficial to communities

NEXT STEPS

This chapter covered basic business structures to help you to determine if a nonprofit classification is best for your altruistic idea. Assuming it is, you are now aware of the options to structure your organization. Note that throughout this book, you might see the nonprofit organization referred to as "your" nonprofit, which is just an easier way to reference the nonprofit that you, the reader, are looking to start. However, if you decide to incorporate as a nonprofit, then, as the founder, the nonprofit is technically not "yours," as it will be run by the Board of Directors.

Subsequent chapters will focus on high level concepts that all nonprofits, regardless of country or business structure will find useful. Now it is time to create your strategic plan, and the next chapter will guide you in doing so.

2

PLANNING YOUR NONPROFIT

By now, you are aware of the different types of nonprofit organizations and are able to decide on a high level as to which type to pursue. Based on this, you can now move away from the broad idea of creating a nonprofit organization and zero in on what you really want to do. Developing a strategic plan helps you summarize at a high level your near-term goals for your nonprofit and serves as the foundation for creating forms needed when you apply for nonprofit status with the government. This chapter will also discuss defining your vision, mission, and organizational values and choosing a name that encompasses these. Finally, you will learn the basics of creating a business plan stipulating how your organization will operate.

STRATEGIC PLANNING

Starting a nonprofit organization is a significant commitment, and it is commendable that you have shown the initiative to serve your community through your nonprofit idea. However, a nonprofit's chance of longevity is greatly increased when its founder has gone beyond "I want to start a nonprofit," to clearly outlining what value the organization will bring. In this section, we will guide you on what elements you need to create a strategic plan that will become the foundation for your successful nonprofit.

The strategic plan is a way to tell the story of your organization. Remember, this document is a projection into the future and should be a living document (i.e., reviewed and updated periodically). So, you will describe where you are coming from, where you currently are, and what you intend to achieve in the next one to three years. This "story" should be written clearly and precisely, ensuring that someone who has never heard about your organization will understand what your nonprofit is all about.

Conducting Research

Is there a one-size-fits-all method for starting a nonprofit organization? Not really, but there are guidelines you can follow to ensure the success of your endeavor. One of the most essential steps is research.

The main challenge that comes with establishing a nonprofit organization is securing funding. This is mainly because of the increasingly huge numbers of existing nonprofits. For example, the United States already hosts more than a million charitable organizations (National Council of Nonprofits, 2014). Such statistics help you to do a quick assessment of the competitive environment that you are about to step into. You must do enough prior research to start on the right footing in such an atmosphere.

Here are ideas for research questions you need to find answers to authentically.

- **Is there a gap that can be filled by your idea?:** You might have the best idea, but is it an answer to the needs of the community that you intend to serve? Be specific on the problems that your nonprofit is more likely to solve. Are there people who have those problems in the community that you are targeting? Also, find out if other nonprofits serve the same purpose and population. If they are there, you should assess their level of financial stability. If you can create a more financially stable nonprofit organization than the currently available ones, you might gain a competitive edge. You might also want to consider collaborating with a fiscal sponsor so that your take-off is more guaranteed.

- **What plans do you have for financing the organization?**: Having people who have a passion that aligns with the nonprofit's mission is good. However, let's face it; you will need money to get and keep the ball rolling. Brainstorm a list of potential donors, research available grants, and study other similar nonprofits to understand how they gain funding. A clear plan for financing will be a crucial component of your business plan and, somewhat counterintuitively, will assist you in attracting funding.

- **What are the startup costs of the organization?**: Here, you have to consider both the major and minor expenses. Will you rent or buy a facility from which the operations will be run? Do not overlook the costs of permits, special licenses, and certifications if your nonprofit will be involved with services such as childcare. As you evaluate the monetary costs, also remember to look at the time-related ones.

- **How will your nonprofit organization demonstrate its positive effects on beneficiaries?**: This question indirectly measures the sustainability of your nonprofit. One of the things that will encourage investors to keep supporting your organization is when you can prove to them that it is exhibiting a positive impact. This means that you should come up with parameters that you will use to evaluate the extent of your impact.

Another way to find out the prospective viability of your nonprofit is to use the effective altruism (EA) strategy. With this method, three major factors are evaluated:

- **Level of neglectedness:** Here, you are looking at whether others have implemented the same idea that you have. Are there any differences or similarities in how you intend to start and run your organization?
- **Evaluation of importance:** In an ideal situation, will your idea have a significant positive impact?
- **Measure of tractability:** Will your organization make it?

Based on your research and answers to the above questions, you can develop a draft of the nonprofit's strategic plan. As time progresses, the strategic plan will be updated with the help of the board of directors. While not required to submit with the application for tax exemption, a strategic plan is important evidence of the long-term viability of the nonprofit and is recommended supplemental material to include. The information also helps you to focus on initial programs/activities and can be used to recruit board members. Here is a list of some of the things that should be covered in your strategic plan document:

- the description and history of the organization
- organizational chart
- currently available and expected resources
- the problem and how programs/activities provide a solution
- key performance indicators (KPI)
- environmental and SWOT (strength, weaknesses, opportunities, threats) analyses
- clear plans on how you will hit the KPIs

Developing Your Activities

Generally, a strategic plan comprises the work planned and intended results. The planned work is made up of the *resources* that you need and the *activities* that you intend to undertake using the inputs. Be sure to list the activities that your organization undertakes in a concise manner. Go straight to the point and avoid vague or broad statements. Please note that specificity does not imply that you should omit some details. In fact, more details bring increased specificity. If, for instance, your organization intends to build a school, the details on the size, location, number of students, and instructors should be clear.

Here are some questions that can give you insights into what you should include concerning the activities of your organization:

- What operations does your organization undertake?
- What are your fundraising plans?
- Where do the activities of your nonprofit organization take place?
- Are you going to employ the services of an intermediary in carrying out your activities?
- What is the link between your organization's activities and its overall purpose?
- Is the organization going to charge its clients a fee? If yes, how much is that?
- Who are your beneficiaries, and are there any specific criteria for selecting them?

Evaluating Programs

A nonprofit organization's results are measured in terms of output, outcome, and impact. If things go according to plan, what outputs do you expect after completing the activities? The *output* is in the form of the services that you want to deliver. The right amount of output will yield certain *outcomes*, which are evaluated as the extent to which the target population benefits. Finally, the outcome is used to assess the *impact* of the initial endeavor, seen through visible expected changes in the lives of the targeted people and the community at large.

Nonprofit organizations regularly undertake research that helps evaluate their programs' effectiveness and impact. These assessments also help them identify areas of improvement. Usually, nonprofit organizations employ the expertise of third parties who can carry out the studies. This strategy is vital in dealing with possible bias if the evaluation is to be done by insiders. However, as a startup nonprofit, a more informal assessment of programs can be completed.

Program evaluation studies fall into two categories, which are:

- **Implementation studies:** These studies are meant to analyze if the program is being implemented according to the set plan.
- **Impact studies:** These studies focus on the effects of the program to see if it is yielding the desired projected impact.

WRITING YOUR VISION AND MISSION STATEMENTS

Both the mission and vision statements describe important aspects of your business. However, these two terms are not synonyms. The mission statement focuses on your organization's aims, objectives, and operations. Simply put, your mission answers the "what" and "who" questions concerning your business. On the other hand, the vision statement explains your business' existence. In other words, your vision statement will tell people about the "why" parts of the mission statement and the business as a whole. The vision statement goes on to iterate the values of your organization as well as its projected future. Stakeholders can see where your organization and the people that it serves are most likely to be in, say, five, ten, or twenty years.

In summary, here are the significant differences between a vision and a mission statement:

- Mission statements focus on the current *status quo*; vision statements project into the future.
- Mission statements give a picture of what the company is now; vision statements give an idea of what the organization will be like in the future.

Examples of Well-Written Vision Statements

Are you wondering how you can best put together an excellent vision statement for your nonprofit? Great examples of vision statements are outlined in this section. Going through these can give you vital insights that you can use in developing your own (Henry, 2017).

- **Alzheimer's Association:** A world without Alzheimer's disease.
- **PAN Foundation:** A nation in which everyone can get the healthcare they need.
- **Mayo Clinic:** Provide an unparalleled experience as the most trusted partner for health care.

- **Oceana:** Our vision is for the oceans to be as rich, healthy, and abundant as they once were.
- **Save the Children:** A world in which every child attains the right to survival, protection, development, and participation.
- **Care International:** A world of hope, tolerance, and social justice, where poverty has been overcome, and all people live in dignity and security.

Examples of Well-Written Mission Statements

As much as mission statements are crucial for your organization's growth and development, putting one together can be difficult, especially if it is the first time you are going through such a process. As a basic template, the mission statement describes WHO you help, what you help them DO, so as to achieve what OUTCOME. Below are good examples that will trigger your brainstorming (GiveForms, 2022):

- **Khan Academy:** Our mission is to provide free, world-class education for anyone, anywhere.
- **Faith Matters Network:** Faith Matters Network catalyzes personal and social change by equipping community organizers, faith leaders, and activists with resources for

connection, spiritual sustainability, and accompaniment.

- **Human Rights Watch:** Human Rights Watch defends the rights of people worldwide.
- **Vancouver Public Library:** Our mission is a free place for everyone to discover, create and share ideas and information.
- **AARP:** AARP's mission is to empower people to choose how they live as they age.

CREATING ORGANIZATIONAL VALUES

By just reading the vision and mission statements of your organization, everyone is able to picture why you exist. The values of your organization are the grand plan that explains how you intend to accomplish your vision and mission and, thereby, impact the world. They are the ones that guide the activities that your company engages in. You can think of your values as boundaries that help you stay within the limits of your territory and do what is expected of you. Therefore, the values of your nonprofit organization define who you are—that is, your brand. Another vital effect of well-stipulated values is that your board members, employees, and volunteers unite toward a common cause that pushes the organization's goals forward.

Let's look at the example of a nonprofit organization called Goodwill. Here are its clearly stipulated values (Raj, 2022):

- **Respect:** We treat all people with dignity and respect.
- **Stewardship:** We honor our heritage by being socially, financially, and environmentally responsible.
- **Ethics:** We strive to meet the highest ethical standards.
- **Learning:** We challenge each other to strive for excellence and to continually learn.
- **Innovation:** We embrace continuous improvement, bold creativity, and change.

Getting Started

Now that you understand the importance of creating values for your organization, the next step is to brainstorm. It is recommended that the more people involved in developing the nonprofit's values, the better. Brainstorming with existing volunteers or team members increases the probability that the values will accurately reflect your organization and gives your team a sense of ownership and accountability. Some of the questions for you to consider, whose answers may indirectly determine the values of your organization, are:

- What are the main considerations on which you base your decisions?
- Which qualities do you expect every person in your organization to possess?
- What are the strengths and weaknesses of your organization?
- What one thing will give you satisfaction if you are remembered for it?
- What does that memorable and fulfilling moment in the organization look like?

Narrow Down What You Have

Once you have finished brainstorming, you will have a list of ideas that will need to be summarized in a more concise manner. You will even need to assess the relevance of the information. To do this, you can ask questions such as these:

- To what extent is this value sustainable? Will it still be relevant in five or ten years to come?
- Does this value apply to the long-term success of this organization?
- To what extent does this idea apply to the organization and its employees?

- Can we apply this to aspects such as donor relations or program development?
- Will this come in handy in our decision-making process, even in the future?

Finalize the Values

Now you have words that concisely describe the values of your organization. For example, words like kindness, integrity, and accountability might be on the list. However, as easy as they are to remember, single words cannot explicitly explain what your organization is all about. You may need to combine a few words in a statement. Therefore, you will need to sit down and discuss the meaning of each word on the refined list. For each word, draft statements describing how it relates to your organization. Doing this helps to avoid certain misinterpretations in the future. Besides, it becomes easier to assess if the value is being adhered to in the manner stipulated in the statements.

CHOOSING A NAME

Do you already have a name for your organization? If not, this section will provide you with relevant insights for choosing an appropriate name for your nonprofit. Generally, you should create a name that is unique to your organization and the activities that are associated with it. Remember, the name of your organization is part of your brand, so carefully coming up with one is of paramount importance. Here are some tips that you can consider:

- Brainstorm.
- Select the names that are more appealing from the brainstorming list. Please, consider names that are more inspiring and memorable at this stage.
- Try to make the name link with your mission, type of activities, or even the location of the organization.
- Create a name that is easy to remember.
- Avoid being too descriptive and using technical jargon.
- It is possible to use abbreviations if you create a good one.

Before finalizing your nonprofit organization name, it is important to check with a domain registration site (for example, NameCheap, Google, or GoDaddy in the United States, the WHOIS directory on the Canadian Internet Registration Authority (CIRA) in Canada, weare.ie in Ireland, Ionos or Nominet in the United Kingdom, the business name check tool on the business.gov.au website) to see if the name is still available (see Chapter 6 for more information on website terminology and creation).

Trademark Search

Once you have a list of potential names, it is crucial to check for trademarks. A trademark is a legally registered phrase, symbol, or word that uniquely represents a company, as well as its products and services, such as a logo or brand name. For instance, the American Red Cross has a trademarked name and a trademarked red cross emblem as its logo.

If you want to search for existing trademarks, here are some important links that might come in handy.

- Australia: https://search.ipaustralia.gov-.au/trademarks/search/quick or https://tmchecker.ipaustralia.gov.au/start
- Canada: https://www.ic.gc.ca/app/opic-cipo/trdmrks/srch/home?lang=eng
- Ireland: https://www.ipoi.gov.ie/en/ip-search-tools/trademark-search/
- United Kingdom: https://www.gov.uk/search-for-trademark
- United States: https://www.uspto.gov/trade-marks/search/using-trademark-electronic-search-system

Trademark Registration

Once you have determined that your desired nonprofit name has not been trademarked, then it is important for you to register the trademark for your use. This is an optional step but recommended because it provides some branding benefits that might interest you. These include:

- **Expansion:** With a federally registered trademark, you put your organization in a position to expand if needed. All you need to do is license your nonprofit's trademark to relevant affiliates.
- **Identification:** When your organization has a federally registered trademark, this becomes its identity that differentiates it from other companies.
- **Value addition:** A federally registered trademark gives more value to your organization. It is more or less like any other asset that your organization has.

An application for registration of a trademark or service mark must accurately state the date on which the mark was first used. The date of first use is the date a registered or unregistered trademark was first used on goods and services offered commercially. For nonprofits, publishing your website using the nonprof it's name as the domain is an acceptable first use on your trademark application.

The actual process to submit a trademark application is a bit involved, but there are clear instructions on the following government websites and some even have instructional videos.

- Australia: https://www.ipaustralia.-gov.au/trade-marks/how-to-apply-for-a-trade-mark
- Canada: https://ised-isde.canada.-ca/site/canadian-intellectual-property-office/en/trademarks/file-new-or-amended-trademark-or-certification-mark-application
- Ireland: https://www.ipoi.gov.ie/en/types-of-ip/trade-marks/the-application-process/guide-to-completing-the-application-form/
- United Kingdom: https://www.gov.uk/how-to-register-a-trade-mark
- United States: https://www.uspto.-gov/trademarks/apply

CREATING A BUSINESS PLAN

At the beginning of the chapter, we reviewed how to complete a strategic plan as a way to communicate the nonprofit's direction, plans, and goals. Another important document to create is a business plan, which describes how the nonprofit's goals will be achieved. A business plan typically looks at finances, people orientation, activities, and management. Your business plan should answer questions such as "what," "who," "why," and "when."

The format of your business plan will largely depend on the audience that you are targeting. However, the general format of most business plans, irrespective of the audience, is outlined below:

- **Table of contents:** This outlines what is included in your business plan.
- **The executive summary:** It gives an overview of the whole business plan. Ideally, state the problem statement, the organization's mission, and the general roadmap to reaching the nonprofit's goal.
- **The people involved:** Here, you mention all board, committee, volunteering, and staff members. Be sure to explain the roles of all the people.

- **Market opportunities:** This is also known as competitive analysis and is informed by research. Find out if other organizations are doing exactly what you want to do. If there are any similarities, you will need to identify them. Also, find out their weaknesses, which are areas of opportunity for your nonprofit.
- **Services and programs:** What services and programs will you undertake? Explain more about how you will implement these plans.
- **Contingencies:** Are there any factors that might change from the current status quo? Identify them so you can plan how to tweak your organization to the change. For example, if there are chances that a particular fundraising project might not be viable, say, in the rainy season, you could put together an alternative money-making project to cater to the possible gap.
- **Financial health:** You can look at the current short-term and long-term analysis of your finances. Your financial projects give insights into the sustainability of your nonprofit organization. Generally, the financial health section should have four major components:

- **Revenue sources:** The activities that your nonprofit will undertake require financial support. How do you intend to generate the money to fund your organization's activities? You must be clear on how much you will get and from where. If there are any fundraising activities, how much money is more likely to come from the endeavor? Are there any government grants that you look forward to receiving?

- **Operation costs:** Your business plan should clearly state the day-to-day costs of running your nonprofit.

- **Program costs:** What programs are you looking forward to undertaking? What are the associated costs?

- **Capital structure:** Running a nonprofit organization is one thing, yet starting it is another. You might project revenue and operation and program costs, but how will you get the ball rolling? How do you intend to raise the money to start funding the initial moves of the business? Will you fund them from your pocket? Are there other people who are willing to help?

NEXT STEPS

This chapter tackled various strategies that form the foundation for your nonprofit organization's take-off. We also explored naming your organization, searching for trademarks, as well as creating your mission and vision statements. To add to creating the foundation of your organization, the next chapter will enlighten you on how to develop a reasonable budget for your organization.

3

DEVELOPING A BUDGET

Nonprofit organizations persistently endeavor to sustain and enhance their functionality. One of the strategies that satisfies this mission is appropriate budgeting. A nonprofit budget is a financial summary used to plan expenditures that you expect in your organization, in addition to distributing expected revenue over a scheduled period. This chapter will identify the process and importance of developing a nonprofit budget.

BUDGETING FOR NONPROFITS

Developing a nonprofit budget is a fundamental planning process for success that is critical for financial management strategy. Working within the guidelines of a budget ensures maximum and efficient utilization of funds, thereby avoiding wasting resources and acquiring debt. Budgeting also helps you monitor the progress of your organization throughout the year.

A well-understood budget offers better feedback and support from the board members, staff, and donors. It also saves time during financial meetings, compared to discussing without documentation of money-related activities. In addition, a budget offers transparency to your Board members, staff, donors, and the general public who may be interested in your organization's operations. Transparency instills trust and confidence in everyone involved, especially donors, who need to know what they are contributing to and if they are making a difference. Finally, a well-prepared budget clearly identifies the programs and initiatives that are and are not performing well. This information helps you to critically prioritize activities that fulfill your nonprofit's mission.

Features of an Effective Nonprofit Budget

An effective nonprofit budget is designed to improve the utilization of limited resources. It also contributes to the proficient satisfaction of your organization's mission by targeting principal objectives. Features that structure a successful nonprofit budget include planning early, being time-conscious, having well-defined activities, involving your team, and using realistic and quantifiable metrics. Here, you will learn how each of these features contributes to the effectiveness of a nonprofit budget.

Plan Early

Nonprofit budgeting is a process that takes time because it requires you to search for relevant information. This information includes deciding on elements to incorporate into your budget, its layout, as well as forecasting and management methods. You also need enough time to consult relevant stakeholders when developing a budget.

Teamwork

First, the process of developing a budget stresses the need to gather input from relevant stakeholders. Second, you present the first draft of your budget to the board. Third, you allow the entire team and donors to familiarize themselves with the budget after getting approval from the board. Involving your board and staff members improves the accuracy and comprehension of a budget.

Be Simple and Precise

Ensure that you clearly name the revenues and expenses in your budget. The budget must not be cluttered. It must be simple and precise while providing sufficient information. This way, the budget is more likely to promote a sound and faster decision-making process by the board members and supporters.

Well-Defined Activities

Your nonprofit budget should be well-formulated to complement your strategic plan. Hence, all activities in the strategic plan should be accounted for in your nonprofit budget. Moreover, separate budgets should be developed for each specific activity or program to ensure that your finances are thoroughly prepared and distributed. Overall, an annual budget is designed by combining all the separate budget components into one fiscal document.

Suppose your organization plans a project to raise $10,000 to construct a library for the community. You will need to organize the allocation of your resources toward building the library. The plan should include estimating the cost of building the library, including books, computers, efficient Wi-Fi, and furniture. You may also include miscellaneous expenses like accounting, legal, and insurance charges. Furthermore, you are required to mention the sources of the resources needed to fund the project.

Realistic and Quantifiable Metrics

You will need to be realistic as you prepare your budget. To avoid basing your budget on assumptions, gather quotations from service providers and partners to help you formulate a budget with real numbers. Making assumptions can be inevitable for beginners, but you can create a reasonable list of estimated expenses. Moreover, you should evaluate your best and worst income-generating setups, but be sure to clearly state the exact sources of funds.

All activities scheduled in the strategic plan should be accounted for in your nonprofit budget, where each source of revenue and expense is allocated a precise sum of money. Realistic and quantifiable metrics are most important when developing a revenue plan for the budget. A well-organized revenue plan should stipulate the amount of money required to complete specific budget components. The way you will raise the needed money should also be clear.

For instance, when your organization is expecting to raise $25,000 from a single fundraising campaign, you can determine the different sources of revenue collection. For example, individual donors will give $5,000, social events will raise $10,000, and $10,000 will be donated by corporations and foundations. Remember, it is encouraged to set aspirational goals to push your team to raise more, but the expected revenue must be realistic and attainable. Otherwise, it may be challenging to raise the necessary amount if it is too high. Setting unattainable revenue goals also increases the risk of experiencing financial deficits while disheartening your team at the same time.

Time Conscience

Whenever you set goals in your strategic plan, they have to be time-specific. A time-based budget considers the time needed to get the budget approved by the board. This ensures that the plan's components are implemented and completed per schedule. Regular reviews should be established with your team to ensure that your organization's activities are funded according to the budget planned and within a specific period.

Time is important to consider when developing a budget, as it helps you decide when to expect and collect revenue and implement planned activities or programs for the organization. For example, when your organization has an expensive project to implement, you can host fundraising campaigns with a high probability of yielding large amounts of income. This money will then be used to fund the expensive project. Hence, timing can help strategize the budget by planning to host fundraising campaigns that produce revenue before project implementation.

TYPES OF NONPROFIT BUDGETS

There are different nonprofit budget types, and each has its specific purpose. To take charge of your finances, you will create two chief budgets for your nonprofit: operating and capital. Cash flow and opportunity budgets are also essential when you want to improve and expand your organization's operations.

Capital Budget

A capital budget is a financial plan that compiles the costs and income needed to implement long-term or expensive projects requiring more than one financial year to fund. A capital budget is also associated with campaigns designed to raise resources to acquire assets for your nonprofit, such as land and buildings. This type of budget can also be used as a strategy to determine if certain large and expensive projects are worth funding.

Operating Budget

An operating budget breaks down the organization's predicted annual expenses and revenue in broad terms. This budget focuses on highlighting your operating expenses into overhead and program expenditures, while also indicating the total funds to be gained. It also separates your revenue according to their specific sources, in addition to highlighting estimated amounts of expected income. Furthermore, this type of budget links the sources of income to the expenses they will be liable for. An operating budget can be used to estimate the finances needed to carry out activities and programs to fulfill your organization's purpose effectively.

Cash Flow Budget

A cash flow budget is a plan that breaks down and predicts the number of costs that should be paid and revenues to be received on a monthly basis. Simply put, a cash flow budget is used to track the amount of money being received and ejected from the organization. Therefore, it is a financial management strategy used to ensure the availability of funds when needed.

Opportunity Budget

This budget is designed as an expansion strategy that invests in the growth of the organization. It involves budgeting unrestricted extra funding and making it available for use in any department. A surplus in the budget allows the nonprofit to invest in future innovations, staff, and other resources.

COMPONENTS OF AN EFFECTIVE NONPROFIT BUDGET

Generally, all budgets are characterized by the realistic estimated amount of expenses to operate a nonprofit and the expected revenue necessary to settle them. Expenses consist of overhead and program costs, and revenue is typically made up of donations and grant funds. Let's explore each of these components in depth.

Revenue Budget

An expected revenue budget is developed by estimating the amount of funding that you anticipate acquiring from each source. Your expected revenue should be broken down according to the sources of funds. Planning ahead for expected income increases the probability of having sufficient funding to accomplish your goals. There are two techniques that you can use to predict your forthcoming revenue, and these are the cutoff and discount methods. Not only do both probability methods improve your forecasting techniques, but they also increase your confidence in planning your budget and activities.

Cutoff Method

This is a tool that is used to predict the probability of the total fundraising income that your organization is likely to acquire. It multiplies the needed funding to run a project by the estimated probability of acquiring the total funding from all sources. For example, if you estimate that you need $12,000 for a project but expect a 90% chance of raising it, then your forecasted revenue budget will be $10,800.

Discount Method

This technique is used when you have multiple sources of revenue with different probabilities of donating their funds toward your campaign. The first step in forecasting the revenue budget using the discount method is to estimate realistic amounts of money that you expect to attain from each fundraising source. Second, you multiply this estimated revenue by the probability percentage that a source is more likely to donate. This gives you the forecasted revenue for each source. Last, you add all the calculated forecasts of revenue for each source to get the total amount of expected revenue.

Let's suppose that you need $12,000 for a project and expect individual donors to contribute $2,000 with a probability of 80%, while foundations give $10,000 with a probability of 70%. Then, you will update the predicted revenue from individual donors to $1,600 ($2,000 multiplied by .80) and that for foundations to $7,000 ($10,000 multiplied by .70). Therefore, the total forecasted revenue will be updated to $8,600 ($1,600 plus $7,000).

Expense Budget

An expense budget is a planned schedule that identifies and forecasts the expenditures needed to support various projects for your nonprofit. An expense budget consists of two major categories, which are overhead and program costs.

Overhead Costs

Overhead costs are expenditures that do not directly serve the purpose of delivering programs or products. They accumulate around the clock as they support the day-to-day operations of an organization. Overhead costs are a combination of administrative and fundraising expenses.

- Administrative expenses - These can either be variable or fixed expenses, which should be separated when planning your nonprofit budget. Fixed expenses are costs that remain constant over a long time, even up to years, such as office rent, insurance, or salaries. Variable expenses are costs that frequently change from one year to another, such as staff benefits and legal fees.

- Fundraising expenses - These are development fees that contribute to the mission of your organization. Fundraising expenses include advertising or marketing your campaign and renting a venue. They are also variable expenses because projects scheduled tend to differ between years.

Program Costs

Program expenses are those that are planned for use to deliver programs that directly serve the purpose of enhancing your organization's mission. For instance, your organization may plan a project that will cost $100,000 to construct hospitals in underdeveloped countries. You will want to invest in medical machines and equipment, computers, stationery, and furniture for the program. A higher proportion of program expenses in your budget is more likely to attract donors because it indicates efficient mission accomplishment.

CREATE AN EFFECTIVE BUDGET

Budgeting is a process that requires certain initiatives for it to yield the best results. When you develop and strategize your budget, bear in mind the features discussed earlier, such as planning, teamwork, and simplicity, that make a budget more effective. In this section, we will provide you with the best process for formulating and managing a nonprofit budget.

Predict Revenue

Formulating a revenue budget is one of the more daunting parts of nonprofit budgeting because it is more difficult to predict. However, there are initiatives you can adopt to make this process easier. The first approach is to organize your expected revenue by source; for example, individuals, fundraising events, corporations, and foundations. Keep in mind that nonprofit organizations can generate profits; those profits just have to be reinvested into programs that support the mission.

Next, grade your projected sources of revenue using letters according to the levels of the most to the least dependable funding sources. For instance, grade A should be awarded to the most dependable source, while B is assigned to the second least dependable until all sources are graded. Remember the discount method; use it along with grading to estimate the probability of receiving the donation as well as the total expected revenue (Antonelli, 2017). You can use the following template of a probability table to help you grade and award probabilities to your financial sources:

Grade	Probability	Explanation
A	81% to 100%	Committed or secured revenue assured through written commitments like a contract or cheque from the donor.
B	61% to 80%	High probability, especially when the donors showed interest in the submitted nonprofit's proposal.
C	41% to 60%	Moderate probability when the proposal has only been submitted.
D	21% to 40%	Low probability when the donation is still in discussion.
E	5% to 20%	Very low probability when the board has not met or submitted their proposal to the donor.

Infer Expenses

Categorize the nonprofit's expenses according to program, administrative, and fundraising expenses. This is important because donors prefer to see the number of their contributions being distributed to directly serve the purpose of your organization's mission. This will increase your chances of having recurring contributions from donors.

Incorporate Salaries

There is a misconception that staff working for nonprofit organizations cannot be compensated. The truth is that board members are not awarded salaries or compensated for their service on the board, but can be reimbursed for travel and meetings. A founder can get paid by transitioning from being a board member to a staff position, such as an Executive Director, and should not hesitate to collect a salary.

Compensation for staff could be in the form of salaries, benefits, insurance fees, or non-monetary payments. Compensations are reasonably determined by assessing a worker's performance. Start planning on getting a salary by including it in the expenses section of your nonprofit budget so that you can account for it and work toward attaining it. However, it is advised to wait for the nonprofit to become self-sustaining before you can expect a salary.

Budget for Unforeseen Situations

The strategy of reserving some money in your budget is an approach that is critical to the long-term survival of your nonprofit organization. Budgeting for unforeseen situations is important in sustaining the organization when it goes through devastating times, such as the outbreak of COVID-19 that hit the globe in 2020. Donations and earned revenue were significantly reduced during this era. A study reported that 90% of the nonprofits in Nevada and West Virginia experienced a reduction in individual donations and cancellation of fundraising events during the COVID-19 pandemic (Nonprofit Education Survey Project, 2021).

Reserving some money can also help the organization pay for expenses when it is experiencing delays in receiving revenue or shortfalls in fundraising campaigns. This surplus must be unrestricted so that it can cater to any debts and financial shortfalls and contribute to operating reserves.

Project Your Cash Flow

It is imperative to determine how your finances will maneuver in and out of the organization, and cash flow is the right tool for determining this. For instance, if your organization expects to acquire revenue months after the expected date to pay its expenses, it will fail to settle its expenses on time. Thus, a cash flow budget gives you the opportunity to prepare for revenue delays and organize alternative ways of raising money to settle expenses on time.

Remember Non-Monetary Donations

Research has discovered that 27% of donors give in-kind donations (Farese, 2020). In-kind contributions are goods or services such as equipment, stationery, office space, security, accounting, advertisement, and volunteer hours provided instead of cash for one of the nonprofit's project budget line-items. Such items should be accounted for at fair market values. A fair market value (FMV) is described as the market price of a service or asset that a buyer is willing to pay a service provider in the absence of market pressures like supply and demand. For example, the value of a volunteer is $24.69 per hour. If your organization has ten volunteers that contribute 12 hours per month, that's $2,962.80, which is added to monthly expenses. Therefore, this amount has to be included in the expenses and revenue projections in the budget.

SCRUTINIZE YOUR NONPROFIT BUDGET

Keep reviewing your budget throughout the fiscal year to monitor and improve the financial functioning of your organization. Reviewing involves establishing regular checks to ensure that your organization's activities do not exceed the budget planned. Many nonprofits practice quick and in-depth regular examinations to review the progress of the organization within a set period of time. Quick analyses are usually conducted on a monthly basis, while in-depth reports are implemented annually and quarterly.

- Monthly reviews - Monthly reviews involve regular inspections of the budget, during which you scrutinize the discrepancies between the predicted and actual revenue attained, in addition to expenses incurred by the organization. These are quick and thorough assessments of budgets for individual projects on a monthly basis. Monthly reviews are aimed at identifying discrepancies in the budget at an early stage in order to explain their existence and develop strategies to correct them.

- Quarterly reviews - This is a systematic approach that assesses your budgeted revenue and expenses for a quarter of the fiscal year and then compares them to the actual figures. Quarterly reviews are used to identify funds that were received, utilized, and unexploited. They also enhance sound decision-making based on the progress reviewed in the budget, such as identifying projects which need upgrading.

- Annual reviews - These are practiced when you are creating the following year's budget by reviewing expenses and revenues that were budgeted in the previous year. This will assist you in determining where the organization's activities abided by or strayed from the budget. Therefore, annual reviews will help you to formulate your predicted expenses and revenues for the succeeding financial year based on the past year's budget.

NONPROFIT BUDGET TEMPLATE

This section will provide a template that can help you structure your nonprofit budget. There are budget templates in Microsoft Excel and tools like Group and Outline that enable you to input detailed line items and then view summary data. You can choose to organize however it makes the most sense to you, but following the principles already discussed. Below is one example that utilizes the grading method described previously:

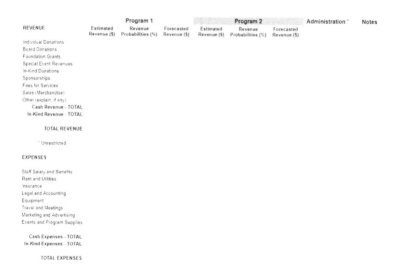

Here is another example that includes forecasted and budgeted amounts with the calculated variance. The numbers shown are fictitious and included only so that you can see how the variance is calculated.

REVENUE	Forecast FY 2022	Budget FY 2023	Variance	Notes
Earned Revenue				
Program Income	$35,000.00	$55,000.00	$20,000.00	
Interest Income	$100.00	$100.00	$0.00	
Total Earned Revenue	$35,100.00	$55,100.00	$20,000.00	
Contributed Revenue				
ABC Foundation	$25,000.00	$25,000.00	$0.00	100% Likely; received award letter
123 Foundation	$10,000.00	$8,000.00	-$2,000.00	80% Likely; long time donor
Foundation Grants	$35,000.00	$33,000.00	-$2,000.00	
Sponsorships	$5,000.00	$5,000.00	$0.00	
Special Events	$0.00	$0.00	$0.00	
Individual Donations	$6,000.00	$7,500.00	$1,500.00	
Board Donations	$2,000.00	$2,000.00	$0.00	
Total Contributed Revenue	$48,000.00	$47,500.00	-$500.00	
TOTAL REVENUE	$83,100.00	$102,600.00	$19,500.00	
EXPENSES				
Staff Salary	$100,000.00	$120,000.00	$20,000.00	
Staff Benefits	$0.00	$0.00	$0.00	
Total Personnel	$100,000.00	$120,000.00	$20,000.00	
Rent and Utilities	$12,000.00	$12,000.00	$0.00	
Insurance	$500.00	$500.00	$0.00	
Legal and Accounting	$0.00	$0.00	$0.00	
Equipment	$0.00	$0.00	$0.00	
Travel and Meetings	$0.00	$0.00	$0.00	
Marketing and Advertising	$200.00	$250.00	$50.00	
Events and Program Supplies	$50.00	$100.00	$50.00	
TOTAL EXPENSES	$112,750.00	$132,850.00	$20,100.00	
Operating Surplus/Deficit	-$29,650.00	-$30,250.00	-$600.00	

A budget that provides the current year and two additional years' projected figures is required to submit with the tax-exempt application, which will be discussed further in Chapter 7. This initial budget will most likely be fine-tuned with the Board of Directors once the startup phase is complete. Here is an example:

Support & Revenue:	Year 1 0%	Year 2 5%	Year 3 5%
Checks			
Cash			
Total Individual Donations			
ABC Foundation			
DEF Foundation			
GHI Foundation			
Total Grants			
In kind Donations			
Sponsorships			
Fees for Services			
Fundraisers			
Sales (Website Merchandise, etc)			
TOTAL:			

Internal & Program Expenses:	Year 1 0%	Year 2 5%	Year 3 5%
Funds Spent On Actual Programs			
Accounting / Bookkeeping			
Fundraising Expenses			
Insurance			
Legal Fees			
Rent (Facilities)			
Office Supplies & Software			
Tax			
Telephone			
Travel			
Training			
Employee Salaries			
TOTAL:	$0	$0	$0
Net Revenue Minus Expenses:	$0	$0	$0

Percentage of Internal Expenses:			
Percentage of Funds Spent on Actual Programs:			

NEXT STEPS

Operating a nonprofit without a budget could expose the organization to devastating outcomes such as overspending, drowning in debt, failing to fulfill its mission, or in worst-case scenarios, forced closure. Not only does a nonprofit budget serve as an important strategy to manage finances that are needed to support programs that fulfill the mission of your organization, but it is also used to attract potential donors. In addition, it strives to ensure the survival of the nonprofit in a changing environment.

The information provided in this chapter guides you into producing a sound nonprofit budget that effectively and efficiently supports the implementation of short-term and long-term goals. Remember, the process of developing a budget involves input from and approval by the board of directors. Therefore, selecting a board is another crucial step in starting a nonprofit organization, which will be dealt with in the next chapter.

4

SELECTING A BOARD

As we have already established in previous chapters, every nonprofit organization is required to have a board of directors that runs its affairs. However, we cannot deny that choosing the wrong people for such a board can have detrimental effects on the ability to accomplish the mission of the organization. Therefore, this chapter is a complete guide to choosing a board that will have the nonprofit's goal at heart.

BOARD RESPONSIBILITIES

A nonprofit organization is only successful if it can achieve its public-service goals as stipulated in its mission statement. Achieving these set goals depends greatly on strategic planning, which we reviewed in Chapter 2 under the assumption that board members were not yet determined. However, if you have board members selected prior to completing the initial planning phase, you can use them to help come up with a viable business strategy founded on identifying opportunities and risks within the nonprofit organization's internal and external environments. The board can then use this knowledge to develop counter-strategies that make the organization successful in delivering its services to target communities.

The main call for the members of the board of a nonprofit organization is to ensure that the mission and vision are being upheld. Moreover, the board should regularly review the mission statement to ensure that it continues to align with the organization's core values and goals. As discussed in the previous chapter, the board is also responsible for regular reviews of the nonprofit's budget. Typically quarterly, this review should enable the board to quickly see what funds were received and how they were utilized. The board then uses this information to refine the direction of the nonprofit, determining the success of projects and fine-tuning spending and fundraising efforts.

Board members, also referred to as directors, should significantly contribute value to the nonprofit organization. This input does not always have to be financial; they might offer their expertise and time. To contribute to raising financial funds, board members should participate in planned fundraising campaigns and advertising endeavors. They may also lead awareness programs that attract donors. In some nonprofit organizations, the board members are obliged to annually contribute certain amounts of money or volunteer a minimum amount of hours. These stipulations will be entered into the organization's bylaws, the creation of which will be discussed in Chapter 5.

BOARD SIZE

Please note that there is no specific number with regard to how many members a nonprofit board should contain. It is recommended to always have an odd number of members so that votes will not result in a tie. Whether a certain number is described as "too many" or "too few" is unique to each organization, based on various factors such as its size and scope. Generally, you need a minimum of three board members to incorporate, but you should validate with state or province-specific guidelines. As the nonprofit organization expands staff, programs, and fundraising efforts, the number of board members may also increase to a range of 12-15, possibly more.

Defining the correct size for your organization can be easier if you can answer the following questions:

- What are the roles and responsibilities that the members of the board should carry out?: Some of the functions of board members are unique to nonprofit organizations, depending on the type of work that they do. In some cases, the roles of the members of the Board of Directors might be governance and administration, while some organizations would rather have a "working board." A governing board might not need too many members to make decision-making easier and less daunting. Decisions are more difficult to make when too many people are involved. Working boards are usually applicable in nonprofit organizations that are run by volunteers. Such boards are more likely to assume many roles, including organizational ones. Such an intense work load is quite time-consuming and may require a relatively large number of board members.
- What skills and experiences are required to fulfill the nonprofit organization's mission?: Creating a board that has a diverse set of skills and experiences is best for any nonprofit organization. You will still need to define the

type of diversity that you require in your organization. Could it be that you want people of different genders or ages? Are you looking for variations in skill sets? Do you want to include proven leaders and those with leadership potential? You have to be clear on what the term "diversity" means to you, as this will help you to decide on the size of your board.

- What number increases the chances of achieving your organization's goals?: The board size may depend on what the nonprofit organization intends to achieve. The goals determine the activities that the organization should engage in. How many members would be enough to spearhead and get those activities going? Sometimes, board members fill in gaps when there is no one available to carry out certain tasks. You have to set up enough board members so these individuals will not be exposed to burnout when such circumstances arise. The good part is that it is possible to increase the size of the board as the organization grows.

- How many members of the board are relevant to maintain the sustainability of the nonprofit?: Ideally, every nonprofit organization should have a president, vice president, secretary, and treasurer. While these are the major positions on the board, sustainability may be compromised if you are to maintain only these. We recommend that you set up your board in such a way that the people who occupy the major positions will mentor others. You might need to increase the size of the board if that is the case. There should be other people who can take over and keep the organization running, even when a member of the board's inner circle is unavailable.

BOARD STRUCTURE

Similar to any for-profit business, the organizational structure of a nonprofit is a key factor in its ability to accomplish its mission. As the nonprofit grows, the board structure will most likely change. For example, committees probably do not yet make sense for a newly formed nonprofit with a small board. However, all boards will have officers, namely a president, vice-president, secretary, and treasurer, that serve an important function in the completion of board responsibilities.

Board Officers

President/Chair Responsibilities

The president or chair is responsible for the overall function of the board, including holding other board members accountable for meeting attendance, committee service, and fundraising. In addition, the president typically sets the agenda for the board meetings and, during the meeting, facilitates it to ensure active participation, adherence to the agenda, and proper voting procedure.

Vice-President/Vice-Chair Responsibilities

The vice president provides a backup to lead board meetings in the absence of the president. This position can also be used as succession planning to ensure knowledge and experience gained by working alongside the president is retained on the board when a president's term expires. In the initial startup phase of your nonprofit, you may not have enough members to elect one to this officer position.

Treasurer Responsibilities

The treasurer is responsible for keeping track of the nonprofit's financial condition, which involves keeping accounting records of all transactions. Along with another board member, usually the board chair, the treasury is the co-signatory on the nonprofit's bank account. The board member in this role also provides key insight into budgeting discussions.

Secretary Responsibilities

The secretary is the board member primarily in charge of communication, ensuring board members are notified of meeting schedules, agendas, minutes, and votes. Validating the organization is operating per bylaws, keeping up-to-date board member contact information, and maintaining the corporate binder are also essential duties of the secretary.

Executive Director

An executive director is hired by the board, but is not a member of the board of directors. However, the founder typically becomes the de facto executive director at the beginning of the nonprofit's existence. An executive director is responsible for all hiring, evaluating, managing, and operational decisions. Executive directors should attend and/or participate in discussions at board meetings. Still, they typically are non-voting members and would leave the room during any vote in which they are directly impacted, such as a salary decision, to avoid the appearance of a conflict of interest. Their presence at board meetings is essential because of their intimate knowledge of the nonprofit's mission, programs, finances, and staff roles and performance.

Committees

Once your board is in place, you should create committees focusing on certain aspects of the organization's operations. This helps to avoid the confusion that comes with involving the whole board in getting things done. Committees are a more structured strategy for practically managing the board's roles. Each selected committee is given responsibility over a certain aspect of management. You can create standing committees whose services are continuous and ongoing. Alternatively, you can set up ad hoc committees that are only active at specific times or events.

Chapter 5 will review the creation of bylaws, where you would spell out the board structure, including committees. However, committees can be set up at any time after the nonprofit is up and running, so it is fine if a committee initially thought to not be needed is added later. The responsibilities of common committees are as follows:

- Governance Committee: As the name suggests, this committee focuses on governance issues. If there is a governance document, such as the organization bylaws, that needs to be altered, they are the ones who do the brainstorming before suggesting recommendations.

- Evaluation Committee: This committee is responsible for coordinating the evaluation of the organization's programs, as well as the board and executive director.
- Finance Committee: This committee reviews the nonprofit's accounting policies and reports in an effort to manage financial risks.
- Fundraising Committee: Board members on this committee work toward creating an overall fundraising strategy to support the nonprofit's mission.
- Nominating Committee: This committee sets up a clear process for recruiting new board members and orienting them so that there is seamless delivery of services.

The committees are governed by what is called a committee charter, which is created by the board. Typical components of a committee charter include:

- a highly descriptive name
- the date when the committee was formed
- clarity on whether the committee is ad hoc or standing
- the powers that are vested upon the committee

- the chair and members of the committee
- the broad purpose of the committee
- the specific tasks of the committee

The following chart depicts an organizational chart similar to what has been described in this section. However, as stated earlier, the initial board might not have committees, or your nonprofit might have different committees. Use this picture as an example to help you understand a potential option.

BOARD CONSIDERATIONS

Influence is one of the more desirable traits for a board member in a nonprofit, but there are many more. Each characteristic determines the skillset and type of mindset that prospective individuals have. While there is no "one-size fits all" method for selecting board members for your nonprofit, we will outline simple criteria you can consider. This will save you from the confusion and work that might come with identifying the most appropriate candidates for your nonprofit's board positions.

One of the reasons why it is vital for you to select the right people is to ensure that the core business of the organization is prioritized and done according to the rules and regulations that govern the nonprofit. There is a huge problem if you incorporate individuals ignorant of the nonprofit's strategy and mission. Stanford did a survey that revealed that approximately 27% of nonprofit organization directors were unhappy with the extent to which their board members understood the organizations' missions and strategies (Meloni, 2021). You do not want your organization to contribute to that 27%. The people you include as part of the board should be positive answers to the questions we compiled in this section.

Do They Work in the Service Industry?

Choose individuals who are relevant to what your organization does. Ideally, ensure each member has qualities and skills complementary to those of others on the board. For example, there is no point in having three attorneys on one board. Instead, include attorneys, accountants, and other skilled professionals who can put different contributions on the table.

Do They Have the Four "Cs"?

There is no doubt that many traits make a good board member for a nonprofit organization, but four are common to all organizations. These are:

- **Community-based**: Board members should belong to communities where they are very active. For example, if you have a board member that is an active member of his small business community and another board member who is involved in her legal community, bringing them together to serve on your nonprofit's board results in an interdependency that will do wonders for the success of the nonprofit. This community involvement contributes to the quality of the decision-making process by the board.
- **Commitment**: The commitment of each board member reflects the overall energy in the board, other internal and external stakeholders, and the whole nonprofit. Choose people who are focused and determined to put in the hard work, time, money, and anything that pushes the organization's mission forward.

- **Curiosity**: Curious board members require less external motivation to do their job. This helps the board channel more energy into getting things done and ensuring that the organization's goals are achieved instead of inspiring individual members.

- **Currency**: Currency can be in the form of monetary, intellectual, social, and network capital. A board member who can bring these various forms of currency to the table is an asset for the organization's progress.

Do They Have Other Commitments?

Board members dedicated to many other commitments outside the nonprofit may find it difficult to put in their best. It is more likely that they will not be able to attend all meetings as scheduled due to the interference of their "other" commitments. If they manage to attend the meetings, the probability that they may not be well-prepared is equally high. Such instances derail the purpose of meetings and the nonprofit as a whole. Therefore, be sure to find out if the prospective candidate has other commitments that may interfere with their commitment to the nonprofit.

Do They Add to the Overall Skill Set of the Board?

Before setting a board, you should have a list of skills that make this team well-rounded, resilient, and formidable. Therefore, when it's time to add new members to the board, you should assess and identify the skills you already have and the ones you still need. Now, look for people who can fill the available gaps in skills within the board.

Do They Possess the Strategic Thinking Acumen?

A great board should reflect a balance between abilities and talent. Experience in governance and being part of a board are vital, but so is thinking outside the box. Exploring new boundaries in terms of ideas and plans will help the board make a difference in the organization. You will always need to improve your strategies for impacting individuals and communities, and this can be impossible if you don't surround yourself with strategic thinkers. It's imperative that you choose board members with the organization's growth in mind.

Can They Cope, Considering the Organization's Size and Growth Stage?

The roles of the board members may slightly differ depending on the size of your organization and its growth stage. For example, a startup organization might not have the capacity to hire more paid staff.

This might mean more hands-on work for the board members to compensate for the inadequacy of paid staff. Does the person you are thinking of match that ability? On the other hand, larger organizations might have more professional staff, so the board might focus on its governance duties. In that case, get board members who have more governance acumen.

Do They Add to Reflecting the Social and Cultural Diversity of the Nonprofit?

Another unique approach to selecting board members for your nonprofit is adding individuals who reflect the people the organization serves. This is a benefit in two ways. First, the board members are motivated to serve their own people. Second, the targeted people trust the nonprofit more because it is run by people to whom they can relate. You need that connection between the nonprofit and the people it serves.

Do They Possess the Three 'Ts'?

Time, treasure, and talent are crucial resources for your organization, which is why board members should feel comfortable offering them. These factors are parameters with which you can measure the prospective candidate's ability to serve your organization and its community. Look for individuals willing to give their time, use their skills and talents, and invest their money to enhance organizational success.

Do They Fulfill the Yin and Yang Principle?

The Yin and Yang principle suggests that everything exists as inseparable and contradictory opposites, like dark versus light, male versus female, or young versus old. Applying this principle to your organization's board would mean that you should get people with contradictory qualities that can complement each other. What one doesn't have, another member will offer. This will increase the cohesiveness of the board while giving room for constructive criticism.

Do They Understand the Organization's Operations?

All nonprofit organizations focus on rendering specific services to targeted individuals or populations. Imagine how effective planning and strategizing would be if board members had an in-depth understanding of the organization's operations. Plans on resource acquisition, logistics, and implementation of objectives are faster and more precise. Let's suppose that your organization helps people who are sick with a certain disease. Then, a nurse could be an effective tool on the board.

BOARD RECRUITMENT

To begin with, you might feel like your only options for board members are your family or friends; however, there is a reason for the saying, "Don't do business w/ friends or family." In fact, there are legal requirements in some areas that prohibit family members from serving on the board. So instead, start by brainstorming what skill set you need on the board (refer back to the previous section on board considerations for guidance).

There is no harm in bringing in business leaders from within the community served by our organization. Such people are laced with influence, which can give your organization some level of authority as it renders its services. For example, for an animal rescue nonprofit, you might want a veterinarian to serve on the board both for the insight he/she could provide into medical costs/treatments, etc., and the community contacts they have. We recommend that you also consider including young professionals who may be eager to make a difference and use board experience for career advancement. Recently retired professionals are another potential source of board members, as they will still have useful contacts and time to commit to the furtherance of the nonprofit's mission. College professors or new parents taking time off from their careers to raise their families may also be interested in serving on the board.

Consider creating a document that summarizes the nonprofit's mission, vision, and board member expectations, such as meeting frequency, term length, and volunteer or donation requirements. It is also a good idea to explain directors and officers insurance, which legally protects board members, and is discussed further in Chapter 9. With this information, you can begin networking with other nonprofits and volunteers. Numerous Facebook groups exist for this very purpose. You can also share the 'board recruitment' document on social and professional networking outlets.

NEXT STEPS

From the information provided in this chapter, it is clear that a well-functioning board is an important component of your nonprofit organization. The organization's board is the connection between its donors, clients, and the community it serves. We discussed how to create an excellent board and the types of committees that you should put in place. The chapter ended by exploring ways to keep board members engaged. The following chapter will focus on how you can best prepare the relevant documents for your organization.

THE POWER OF A BREAK

"I always wondered why somebody doesn't do something about that. Then I realized I was somebody."

— *LILY TOMLIN*

You're taking in a lot of information here, so let's take a moment to reflect on how far you've come. Breaks are important no matter what you're doing, and I'd like to encourage you to take them throughout the process of setting up your non-profit organization. It's easy to feel like you're slacking when you know there's so much still to be done, but short, regular breaks will keep you fresh and on task – and trust me, you'll be far more productive as a result.

Take a moment to consider where you were at the start of this journey, and where you are now. You picked up this book because you wanted guidance. You may have felt overwhelmed by everything you needed to do to get your organization off the ground, or perhaps you didn't feel confident about your capabilities.

As you continue your journey through this book, you'll pick up everything you need to know to make your non-profit dream a reality… You're making astounding progress already.

Before we jump back in, I'd like to ask you to take a moment to help out others who find themselves in the same position. Simply knowing there are resources out there to help could make a world of difference to someone still unsure about whether they have what it takes to start a non-profit.

Don't panic – I'm not asking you to make your workload even heavier. All it will take is a few minutes of your time.

By leaving a review of this book on Amazon, you'll show new readers where they can find exactly the guidance they need to bring their non-profit dream to life.

Simply by letting other readers know how this book has helped you and what they'll find inside it, you'll create a signpost showing them where to find the information they need… Not only will you be starting your own non-profit organization; you'll be helping another one get off the ground too.

Thank you so much for your support. I know how overwhelming it can be when you're starting out, and I want to make this journey as easy for others as I can.

5

PREPARING ORGANIZATION DOCUMENTS

While others seek the services of professionals to assist them in all filings required for them to start their nonprofit, you can do these things on your own and perfectly, too. In this chapter, we will describe how you can best prepare the documents that are required before you kick-start activities in your nonprofit. We will look at the articles of incorporation, bylaws, government registration numbers, and conflict of interest policies. This chapter focuses on requirements for new nonprofits in the United States; however, information specific to nonprofits in Australia, Canada, Ireland, and the United Kingdom is found in Appendices B, C, D, and E, respectively.

CREATING ARTICLES OF INCORPORATION

Generally, the first step in starting your nonprofit is registering the name you intend to give your nonprofit organization, which we reviewed in Chapter 2. After that, you should file the articles of incorporation, which is also known as the Certificate of Incorporation. The articles of incorporation are documents required by the government to endorse the legal existence of an organization. These documents clearly specify your organization's purpose and provide a foundation for the application for tax exemption. Drafting the documents, submitting them to the government, and getting approval is described as incorporation. The focus of this section is to take you through the process of filing for Articles of Incorporation in different countries. One of the common aspects in all these countries is that once the incorporation process is complete, you should strive to maintain a good corporation status by complying with annual or biannual filings.

Legal requirements for creating a nonprofit differ between states. Therefore, it is recommended that you approach your state association of nonprofits so that you get relevant and specific information. For example, some states refer to the articles of incorporation as the certificates of formation, 501 (c)(3) articles of incorporation, or charter documents.

You may also be required to provide proof of corporate name, a certificate of disclosure, and filing fees. In addition, many states stipulate the number of times you should publish the articles of incorporation in a local newspaper. Therefore, you should file the proof of publication with the relevant state agency.

Before you file your application for the articles of incorporation, be sure to include the step-by-step components outlined below.

- **The nonprofit entity's name:** You might be required to add designators such as Inc. or Corp in some states. In some areas, all nonprofit organizations are regarded as corporations, so there won't be a need to add the designator Corp to its name. Please find out the requirements of your state in this regard.
- **Your organization's nature:** Here, you should stipulate that you are a nonprofit organization solely oriented toward public benefit. There are three things that you should clearly mention. First, highlight that your organization's existence is only for charitable causes. Also, stipulate that the organization's funds will never be used for personal use. Last, it should be clear that in the event of the organization's

dissolution, its assets will not be distributed among the directors or owners.

- **The nonprofit's office address:** The address of the nonprofit's head office should be mentioned. You are allowed to add a virtual address, especially if you want the organization to go global. The same applies when you want to avoid having a permanent address, even within the same state. Please, note that many states do not allow you to use "P.O. Box."

- **The registered agent's contact details:** The individual who receives your nonprofit organization's documents on its behalf is whom we are referring to as the registered agent. The primary address of this person is needed in the application so that they can receive relevant documents such as annual reports. A nonprofit officer can act as the registered agent, so in such cases, the address may be the same as that for the head office.

- **The nonprofit's duration:** You should mention the time frame during which your organization will operate. If your organization has no expiration date, you can note that it is perennial or perpetual.

- **The contact information of incorporators:** Incorporators are the undersigned individuals responsible for repairing the article and registering it with the government. Your organization can have more than one incorporator. The names, signatures, and contact details of these people should be included in your application.

- **The Board of Directors' contact details:** The names and addresses of the members of the nonprofit's board should be included. It is possible to change the names of the Board of Directors you initially submitted later. However, you must submit a restated incorporation article to do that.

- **The nonprofit's purpose statement:** This is a statement that mentions the primary goal of your nonprofit. The language that you should use for writing your purpose statement should resemble the one stipulated by the IRS, which says, *"Said corporation is organized exclusively for charitable, religious, educational, and scientific purposes, including, for such purposes, the making of distributions to organizations that qualify as exempt organizations under section 501(c)(3) of the Internal Revenue Code, or the corresponding section of any future federal tax code"* (Hanif, 2022).

- **Any additional members:** Some nonprofits prefer a structure where there are other people, like trustees, whom they include in their decision-making process. You are expected to mention such people when you apply for the articles of incorporation. However, it is usually better to keep decision-making within the board's jurisdiction.

- **More highlights on the organization's standing:** As mentioned earlier, the IRS wants you to confirm that you qualify for tax exemption. Demonstrate that you are not a for-profit organization and will stay within the limits of the activities legally associated with your nonprofit. Mention that the 501c3 rules will be followed regarding distributing the organization's assets upon dissolution. The following wording is recommended, *"Upon the dissolution of this organization, assets shall be distributed for one or more exempt purposes within the meaning of section 501(c)(3) of the Internal Revenue Code, or corresponding section of any future federal tax code, or shall be distributed to the federal government, or to a state or local government, for a public purpose"* (IRS.gov, 2020).

DOCUMENTING BYLAWS

You can think of nonprofit bylaws as the manual or governing document for operating the organization. The board creates the bylaws for your organization, which are not meant to replace but supplement the regulations stipulated by the local corporate code. In other words, nonprofit bylaws should comply with rules the government already sets regarding charitable organizations.

The main reason nonprofit bylaws are set is to guide the decision-making process and actions of the organization's board. These laws also help avoid conflicts, but they can be reasonably resolved if they do happen. Nonprofit bylaws also define the boundaries of authority, powers, actions, and rights by clearly stating what is expected of every organization member.

The Master Checklist

There are some things that you should never leave out when you draft the bylaws for your organization, and these include the following.

- **The organization's name and purpose:** The name of the organization can be stated in the title of the document. You might not need to mention the organization's purpose again if it is already expressed in the articles of association.

- **Board members and officers:** The bylaws should clearly state how these stakeholders are elected and their roles and terms of office. It is recommended to stagger board terms so that the entire board does not turn over simultaneously. So, for example, some board members can be elected to one-year terms, some to two-year terms, and some to three-year terms. Also, review state or province guidelines to ensure minimum and maximum term length requirements are incorporated.

- **The structure of the board:** Here, you will define the size of your board. Be sure to mention the minimum and maximum numbers and any standing committees that should be part of the organization. It is also helpful to note how emergency board meetings can be decided and carried out.

- **The board members' indemnification and compensation:** Indemnity refers to the protection given to board members from possible harm or loss as they deliver on their duties. When you are allowed to do so, it is imperative that you put these protection measures in place. In addition, any compensation arrangements for employees, officers, and directors should be clearly stated, and approval should adhere to the appropriate language according to IRS Form 1023.

- **The chief executive's role:** The nonprofit board can hire a chief executive officer who oversees the running of the organization on a daily basis. The procedures for hiring and terminating the services of the individual should also be clearly stipulated. There should also be a rule mentioning the minimum number of votes required to implement termination decisions.

- **Membership:** What are the regulations around membership in your organization? Could it be that individuals who are part of the Board of Directors are the only members? If there are other people, how is their membership defined? So, you will look at eligibility issues, voting rights, dues, and termination guidelines.

- **Guidelines for meetings:** The bylaws should highlight how many meetings should be held, as well as the quorum, which is the minimum number of board members that must be present when official decisions are made. So, how many board members can make a decision valid should be clear.

- **Amendments:** We recommend that you make amending the bylaws simple enough, as the changes usually improve the running of the organization. For instance, you could allow amendments at board meetings based on a majority rule.
- **Dissolution:** Including a dissolution clause is a requirement for nonprofit organizations unless the law states otherwise. In the clause, mention that the nonprofit's assets will be distributed for tax-exempt purposes.

Tips on Nonprofit Bylaws

Suggested best practices for nonprofit bylaws are as follows.

- Publicize the nonprofit's bylaws to enhance transparency and accountability, which are great strategies for attracting donors and appropriate beneficiaries.
- When you are putting together bylaws for your organization, stick to fundamental regulations relevant to the organization's running. Leave out information that can easily change, such as job descriptions.

- Customize the bylaws to align with the nonprofit's mission, operational needs, and goals.
- Ensure you are clear on the differences between "may" and "shall" as you draft the bylaws. For example, the term "shall" makes things mandatory, while "may" makes them optional.
- Be realistic and refrain from being too ambitious. It is better to leave out rules that are unlikely to be adhered to.
- Regularly review the bylaws.

DEVELOPING A CONFLICT OF INTEREST POLICY

The conflict of interest policy is one of the most crucial in a nonprofit and should be reviewed by the board regularly. This policy should exist in writing. In addition, a signed conflict of interest for each board member should be on file, and copies should be included in the tax-exempt application. Please note that failure to manage conflicts may result in penalties referred to as "intermediate sanctions." These sanctions affect the person who may be benefiting from acting against the nonprofit's and the organization's best interests.

In some states, nonprofit organizations must follow pre-drafted guidelines for a conflict of interest policy. For instance, in New York, nonprofit organizations are guided on what they should include in their policies, including a clause that the employees and management are to do things in the "best interest of the nonprofit" (National Council of Nonprofits, 2014). However, if your state does not necessarily provide a guide for drafting a conflict of interest policy, check the list below for some of the nuggets that you should include:

- that those who actually or assume that they have a conflict disclose the disagreement
- to prohibit voting by board members on matters that involve conflicts
- how certain conflicts should be managed
- the procedures for determining if there are conflicts of interest between board members

In cases where the executive director has a seat on the board, the conflict of interest policy should also state when it is necessary for any board member, including the executive director, to recuse themselves from specific votes or discussions where a conflict of interest might exist.

Some Pointers

Quite often, directors and other employees may be unaware that their actions contradict the organization's best interests. Therefore, it is the role of the nonprofit to put in place procedures directed toward raising awareness and enlightening its stakeholders in this regard. Organization members should also be encouraged to disclose any conflicts of interest. Additionally, your organization can stay at the top of the game if the following is done:

- The board allocates time, at least once a year, to discuss the possible scenarios that reflect potential conflicts of interest and how these situations can be best managed.
- If "conflicts of interest" were addressed before, minutes should be kept, and how the issue was solved should be clearly explained.
- The nonprofit organization can distribute a questionnaire that helps board members, and other employees disclose conflicts of interest.

DEVELOPING A SEXUAL HARASSMENT POLICY

All organizations should have a sexual harassment policy to protect their employees and volunteers. While most states do not require a written policy before incorporation, creating one is still recommended prior to offering services to the public. A harassment scandal hurts not only its direct victims but also an organization's reputation, which is what builds public trust and ensures its success.

This policy should exist in writing, and a copy should be included in the tax-exempt application. The following sections are recommended:

- **Policy Statement**: summarizes the organization's commitment to fostering an environment free of harassment.

"[Organization name] is committed to providing a safe environment for all its employees free from discrimination on any grounds and harassment at work, including sexual harassment. [Organization name] will operate a zero-tolerance policy for any form of sexual harassment in the workplace, treat all incidents seriously, and promptly investigate all allegations of sexual harassment. Any person found to have sexually harassed another will face disciplinary action, up to and including dismissal from employment. All complaints of sexual harassment will be taken seriously and treated with respect and in confi-

dence. No one will be victimized for making such a complaint."

- **Definition**: includes an explanation of what constitutes sexual harassment at a high level and specific examples (for example, physical, verbal, and non-verbal).
- **Complaints Procedure:** clearly defines how a complaint should be escalated. Will there be a designated employee/volunteer at the organization that will listen to and log complaints? How is this information communicated to the organization's employees, volunteers, donors, and visitors? When a complaint is received, define how it will be logged and what information will be collected. Provide an opportunity for the victim to log informally or formally.
- **Disciplinary Measures:** documents the penalty for someone in the organization who is found to have sexually harassed another under the terms of the policy.
- **Education Process:** communicates specifics on how the organization plans to train the people who work for and support it. Training should include compliance aspects, which explain all of

the information from previous bullet points, as well as sensitivity and, potentially, bystander intervention training. Some states, like California, require regular and legally compliant harassment and prevention training for organizations that have over 50 employees. Even if formal training is not provided, document how the policy and its specifics will be disseminated.

- **Policy Evaluation:** explains how the policy will be reviewed for success and revised, as needed. This section might also include the regular administration of a confidential survey. This survey promotes a healthy working environment by enabling all members of the organization (for example, board, employees, volunteers, and visitors) to express their thoughts about whether harassment is occurring and, if so, how severe a problem it is. Survey results also provide important data to effectively evaluate the policy and see where improvements can be made.

DEFINING ACTIVITIES

As described in previous chapters, starting a nonprofit, like any business, requires a clear definition of a vision, mission, and activities. In preparation for the tax-exempt application, it is essential to create a narrative description of these aspects of the nonprofit. Most of this information you have already developed in your business and strategic plans that were explained in Chapter 2. There is no set template for the narrative, but it is recommended that the following elements be included:

- **Organization Overview**: Include the overall purpose of the organization, the founder's experience/background, why it started, what need will be filled (specifically, what are you providing that other existing nonprofits cannot), and what benefit will be provided to the community.

- **Mission, Vision, Values**: Provide details on the organization's mission, vision, and values and how the mission will be accomplished. For example, if you are starting an animal rescue, what will be the "qualifications" for animals rescued? Will the organization focus on a specific type of animal, breed, or age? Where will animals be saved from? Will animals be fostered and then adopted out? Will the amount spent on veterinary expenses be limited?

- **Program Summary**: Explain what programs will be offered and what percentage of the budget will be allocated to each program.
- **Operations**: Describe whether the organization will initially be run by volunteers or staff. Share any organizational charts and employee/volunteering recruitment plans.
- **Revenue Sources**: State at a high level how programs will be funded. For example, will there be a charge for services? Will the organization apply for grants or rely on general public donations? What percentage of funds will be allocated to programs versus administrative functions? Note that budget specifics will be referenced in the accompanying budget.
- **Marketing**: Summarize the marketing plan. Is the website created? What social media outlets will be utilized? Is there a plan to provide a press release?

APPLYING FOR A REGISTRATION NUMBER

Even though nonprofit organizations are not run to earn profits, they are still expected to possess an employer identification number (EIN) because they are in business. You can think of the EIN as your organization's Social Security number. Sometimes, the EIN is also called the tax identification number (TIN) or the federal employer identification number (FEIN).

Irrespective of whether your nonprofit has employees or depends on volunteers, it must possess an EIN. As a business, the nonprofit must file tax forms. It may also need to apply for business loans, pay payroll taxes, open a business bank account, or apply for local business permits and licenses.

When your organization is recognized as a legal nonprofit in your state, you can apply for the EIN. You will use this number when you apply for federal tax exemption. The EIN can be included in the header or footer of each of the documents explained in this chapter as an identifier when submitting the tax-exempt application to the federal government. The person who applies for your organization's EIN should have their own social security number, the nonprofit's legal name, as well as physical and mailing addresses. Applying for your organization's EIN can be done online from the IRS website, or you can download IRS Form SS-4, print and complete the form and send it by mail or fax.

Please take note of this **warning** from the IRS (IRS, n.d.):

> *"Don't apply for an EIN until your organization is legally formed. Nearly all organizations are subject to automatic revocation of their tax-exempt status if they fail to file a required return or notice for three consecutive years. When you apply for an EIN, we presume you're legally formed, and the clock starts running on this three-year period."*

NEXT STEPS

By now, you have attained vast knowledge about the documents that you need as you start your nonprofit organization. We also looked at how best you can set up important policies, such as the one for managing conflicts of interest. Once your necessary documentation is in place, you need to set up an online presence, and the next chapter will guide you on how to get that done.

6

SETTING UP AN ONLINE PRESENCE

A n online presence is significantly beneficial for nonprofits when they want to improve their revenue or operations. Recent statistics highlighted a 12.1% increase in online donations and a 50% growth in mobile transactions (Ensor, 2022). Participating in social media networks is an initiative adopted by most organizations, if not all, to adjust to the constantly changing world dominated by technology and media coverage. Today's and future donors are always cruising online, and coming across your nonprofit website could be beneficial. This chapter will discuss the importance of an online presence for nonprofits.

SOCIAL NETWORKING FOR NONPROFITS

An online presence can be set up on various platforms such as websites, articles, newsletters, blog posts, email lists, magazines, and applications. Your organization can use any of these platforms to broaden its audience and sources of donations. One of the significant benefits of creating an online presence is the feasibility of marketing your nonprofit at little cost. All types and sizes of organizations have been able to inform and interact with people on a global scale using the internet. Technology offers an opportunity to produce original and creative ways for the organization to engage with its community. Your organization becomes unique among other nonprofits and leverages this advantage to compete for donations. Let's explore the importance of online social networking in depth.

Gaining Financial Support

Online platforms such as email lists and newsletters are used to constantly keep donors and members informed about the nonprofit's achievements as a result of the donations that it has received. Your online publications should also provide clear guidelines on how people can support your organization. In addition to highlighting what has already been achieved, these publications also underscore the problems that still need to be addressed to further fulfill the organiza-tion's purpose. Hence, these publications will be embedded with appeals for more donations or support to solve present and future problems. Furthermore, social media can be used to connect with new people in need of your help. Creating groups and channels on social media offers an opportunity for your organiza-tion to share grievances and possible solutions with the world.

Celebrating Success

Many publications and social media platforms are leveraged to showcase the achievements of various volunteers, donors, and members. Appreciating your supporters creates a sense of belonging that motivates them to contribute regularly. Instilling a sense of belonging through appreciation welcomes and inspires new audiences to support you.

Driving Change

The first step to driving change is educating people. Education is achieved by publishing in-depth informa-tion that stresses the importance of conducting specific projects to solve problems faced by the community. Moreover, you can share the impact of your organiza-tion and its accomplishments. Such information will inspire individuals, groups, and companies to support your organization. Your online audience will also gain awareness and the power to make educated decisions.

CREATING A WEBSITE

A website is a series of connected internet pages produced for a single organization and situated under the same domain name. Most people use the internet to gain information. This includes people searching for your organization on the internet to understand its intentions and impacts. If your organization's information is not on the internet, people are inclined to question its existence. What could be a better way of targeting new members or donors than to create an internet presence?

This section assumes that you or someone else in your organization will create the website. Most of the options listed are relatively easy to do on your own. However, you could contact a local community college or high school if you feel technologically challenged. Many have programs that partner with small businesses and nonprofits that can help. The students get real-world experience and are able to build a portfolio, while you get something you need for the nonprofit. Another idea is to use freelance websites like fiverr.com that enable you to post a website creation project that would be completed less expensively than with a professional website development company. Keep in mind, though, that you will have to maintain the website and it is beneficial to have a working knowledge of how to update the files.

Choose a Hosting Solution

Hosting companies are used to store all of the files, text, and images that comprise your website. Think of this as your physical home or business storefront. When searching for a hosting company, you should consider the uptime percentage, which is a measure of the dependability and reliability of your site. You want to choose a company with as close to 100% uptime as possible. Other considerations include bandwidth and customer support.

Most web hosting companies also provide an email address with your domain name (for example, "yourname@yourdomain.com" vs. "yourname@gmail.com"). There are numerous reliable hosting solution providers, such as Bluehost, SiteGround, and Cloudways. Other companies, such as Microsoft Azure, Amazon AWS, or DreamHost, provide free hosting for nonprofit organizations. To make your final decision, you can look at customer feedback for hosting companies on popular review websites like Trustpilot and G2 Reviews.

Find a Domain Name

A domain name for your nonprofit directs people to your site. You can think of this as the postal address of your home or business. Hosts offer domain names at a cost. When you choose a domain name, your host registers it and uses it to develop a home page address for your website that is accessible online. We spoke about trademarks in Chapter 2 when determining your nonprofit name. Hopefully, you completed this step before finalizing your name, but if you still need to, please complete a domain search now to ensure that your name is available.

The format of a nonprofit website domain is www.yournonprofitname.org. The domain extension enables users to understand your business better (for example, .org is for nonprofits and .edu is for educational institutions). Note that in countries other than the United States, you may have a country-specific designation after the .org (for example, .au in Australia, .ca in Canada, .ie in Ireland, or .uk in the United Kingdom). New domain extensions are released occasionally, so you should keep informed of any that might make sense for your nonprofit niche, like .yoga for a yoga studio.

Provided you have the budget to purchase more than one domain name, it is a recommended investment that provides brand protection and security. For example, you might also want to buy the .com extension to ensure that your targeted community finds your website and not a different organization. Consider thinking about other ways your name could be spelled (for example, phonetically or common misspellings). You can also register those and have them redirected to your site to ensure you do not lose that website traffic.

Choose a Website Builder

Most hosting companies, such as GoDaddy, Wix, WordPress, Squarespace, and Weebly, will also provide website building capabilities. To aid you in the decision of which website builder will work best for your nonprofit, you should consider the following factors:

- Software Features - Most popular choices include basic software options that enable you to build a suitable website. However, some companies, such as Shopify and Squarespace, have world-class shopping cart solutions, which would be useful if your nonprofit sells items online. Other companies have superior stock images and photo editing tools.
- Templates - Browse the available templates to help choose a website building company. The template includes your website's menus, colors, background elements, and photo and text

alignment. Some companies, such as Wix, offer fewer free ones, but the ones they offer are of superior quality.

- Cost - Generally, it is recommended that you use a paid platform so you can connect to your domain and remove any ads. Website ads typically make a website look less professional and may not align with your nonprofit values. You will also receive more storage, bandwidth, and development tools that outweigh the initial investment.

- Reputation - To ensure that you choose a website builder that will remain in business, look at how long the company has been in business and any industry awards they have received.

- Search Capabilities - To ensure that your website displays as one of the top options when a potential visitor, donor, or client searches for your nonprofit name or related keywords, you need to be aware of search engine optimization (SEO). Some items that increase your website's search engine rankings are the ability to edit title tags and add alt image attributes, keyword tools, automated sitemaps, and search-friendly URLs (for example, yournonprofit-name.org/about versus yournonprofitname.org/34567). Validate that the website builder you are considering provides the above SEO options.

Plan Website Design

Before you begin creating web pages, give yourself adequate time to strategize the website design and content that reflects your organization's mission. Your content should be outlined using elements commonly found on websites. This refers to the five recommended pages for a nonprofit website - Home, About Us, Programs and Services, Support/Donate, and Contact Us. They are your key navigation links that should not be buried or scattered within the body text of the site.

Home Page

The Home page should define your target audience. It should appeal to the user and give them a reason to keep browsing your site. Donor reviews concerning your programs and stories about the nonprofit's impact could appear on this page. The home page should act as a guide to acquiring information from the website.

About Us Page

The About Us page describes the intentions of your nonprofit in terms of its mission, vision, values, and goals. This page builds credibility by advertising realistic information about your organization. It is a chance to present your unique motivational story and the importance of your mission. On this page, you will define the problems the organization aims to solve and the projected impact of the nonprofit on its target audience. Furthermore, it expands on the importance and benefits of solving the problems to influence the reader to donate.

Programs and Services Page

The Programs and Services page provides clear statements of your organization's goals. The page clearly defines what the programs and services are targeting. It gives a specific schedule of your programs and services.

Support Us Page

The Support Us page is designed to explain the donation process and assure the security of the procedure. It should have an embedded donation form or button. In addition to embedding a donation option, visitors also get information on alternative ways to support your organization, such as passive giving through Altruisto or Humble Bundle. Furthermore, the page informs your website visitors about the impacts of their contributions. It is helpful to include testimonials and stories from the people you have helped. You could also provide a list of how much money it costs to provide your programs. For example, if you have an animal rescue nonprofit, you can share how much it costs to feed an animal for a month and provide veterinary care.

Contact Us Page

The Contact Us page highlights all the options people have to reach your organization. You should provide correct and accessible contact details. Inform your visitors about how and when you intend to respond to their messages.

Create Content

Creating content for your website pages would be the next stage. Use information such as the target audience and the purpose of your website to determine relevant material to incorporate. For example, the purpose of your website could be to promote your fundraising events, keep your audience informed, or recruit new members, volunteers, and donors. Moreover, your content should produce a website with good characteristics. Here are the characteristics of an ideal website.

Functionality and Ease of Use

Your website should be easy and quick to find on the internet. Users who struggle or take more time to access basic information typically exit the website in less than 15 seconds. This means that everything should be accessed within two clicks. Ensure that you produce functional links and avoid embedding broken or dead links, which can impede visitors from accessing important information.

Device Compatibility

Ensure that your website is user-friendly on any device so your audience can access it from anywhere. For example, more than half of people use their smartphones rather than desktops or tablets to access the internet. Hence, your website should function and look the same on any device.

Simplicity and Consistency

Avoid using irrelevant and complex designs or words that make your website difficult for the user to navigate or understand. Huge amounts of text can be off-putting, which makes navigation frustrating. Instead, use short, precise, and simple sentences that are easy to understand. Eliminate irrelevant pop-up advertisements that can overwhelm your site visitors and distract them from the purpose of your website. The layout of your website should be consistent in terms of colors and font styles that match throughout the website. Font styles and sizes should also be easy to read.

Quality Content

Your website should strive to represent your organization with dignity. Good quality content should display your organization's mission, vision, values, and goals. The site should provide sufficient updates about the programs that have been done, especially about the success and progress toward serving your organization's mission. When relevant, insert a reasonable amount of internal links to refer your users to more information.

Attractiveness

Using visual elements can be a way of reducing huge amounts of text. Images, videos, graphs, and charts are visual elements that can convey volumes of information about your organization and mesmerize your web visitors. In addition, upload illustrations that are clear and of good quality. The Aberdeen Group stated that using visual illustrations resulted in businesses increasing their annual revenues by 83% (2016).

Accessibility

Accessibility refers to ensuring your nonprofit's website is equally available to people with disabilities. Paying attention to accessibility features on a website typically generates a better-coded, more robust website that ranks higher in search engines. Therefore, it is important to consider the following accessibility concepts.

- Formatting - Utilize simple language, break information into sections with headings, and use bulleted lists, as applicable.
- Readability - Ensure contrast in color and text, do not use all capital headings, left align text, and use sans serif fonts.
- Images and graphics - Do not auto-play videos, allow users to stop any on-screen animation, and add "alt-text" to all images, video, and audio, which is a textual explanation of a visual element that screen reader software uses.
- Links - Keep links underlined, warn users if a link will open a new tab or file, and write unique link text.

Easy Donation Process

Make donating easy by embedding a one-click donate button on every page or in your website menu header. The donation process should cater to all donors by offering various online payment methods that range from digital wallets, such as PayPal, Apple Pay, or Google Pay to bank transfer payments. Your donation pages should gather relevant donor and donation information using digital forms. Donation forms should be simple, easy, and quick to complete with a few steps.

Digital forms can be embedded or designed to pop up on your online pages. Embedded forms are installed on the donation page of your website. They are associated with a link address that directs the visitor to a donation page. Pop-up forms should be available on every page of your website or social media account. They allow visitors to donate quickly without redirecting them to a donation page. Pop-up forms also make it easy to build your mailing list.

Build Your Mailing List

Calls to action (CTA) elements should be on every page of your website. They should be modest yet eye-catching. To increase the number of subscribers to your mailing list, use CTAs as pop-up forms. Pop-up forms are designed to quickly capture the donor's name and email address for subscriptions. Adding a "join our mailing list" button to every website page is another way of getting people to subscribe. Mailing lists are vital in creating a consistent dialogue between your organization and its members.

Maintain Your Website

An important aspect that makes your website user-friendly and trending is frequently updating it.

Updating the website ensures that its contents load faster, improves the quality of your visuals, and prevents hacks. Hacked sites compromise the trust and security of your visitors' information. This can deter users from visiting your site. You can increase traffic to your website by also updating old posts, such as testimonials and achievements.

An impressively constructed website is characterized by a low bounce rate. A bounce rate is described as the amount of time internet users spend browsing through your web page. A low bounce rate indicates that the website has captured the user's attention because of the accessibility of information. You can assess the bounce rate for your website by opening the Google Analytics Dashboard and clicking the "Audience Overview" option.

DONATION COLLECTION TIPS

You need to design a system that allows your organization to collect online donations on all your online platforms, as well as store and manage donor or donation information. The management system should also ensure that your donor's information is secure. Consider practicing the tips discussed in this section to modify your processes for collecting donations.

Enable Online Donations

Collecting donations online requires a donation form, which you can create for general donations and specific fundraising campaigns. Obviously, the nonprofit needs a bank account to accept donations, which is reviewed in Chapter 9. However, during website creation, you will want to consider how to ask for donations online and what payment processor you want to use.

Online donation forms should be simple, only collect the necessary donor information, and include various donation amounts to reduce donor drop-off rates. Typically, there are two donation forms to choose from: embedded and pop-up forms. Embedded forms are located directly on a website page, presumably the Support Us/Donation page. This type of donation form enables the nonprofit to provide details about its mission, programs, and impact, as well as collect donor names, addresses, emails, and program interests.

Pop-up forms do not have space to include nonprofit information and are used to capture online donations from those that know they want to donate. They can be effective when attached to a website visitor's action, like arriving or leaving the website. It is also recommended to include a Donate button in your website header menu, so it is accessible from any page on your website, and this button can link directly to the donation pop-up form.

Once you determine where to use embedded and pop-up forms on your website, you will need to choose a payment processing system such as PayPal or Stripe. Payment processors allow donors to use credit or debit cards, bank transfers, and digital wallets. All payment processors will charge a fee, but most will enable you to ask donors if they want to increase their donation amount to cover this cost. As it is recommended to set up your website, at least in a basic form, prior to submitting tax exemption paperwork, the selected payment processor most likely will not offer the reduced nonprofit processing fees. You can always change to a different payment processor after you receive official nonprofit tax-exempt status and can provide proof to the payment processor. You may also choose to utilize a donor management system, such as JustGiving and Raisely in Australia, CanadaHelps and Trellis in Canada, Enthuse and iDonate in Ireland, JustGiving and Givey in the United Kingdom, and Donorbox and Givebutter in the United States, that helps the nonprofit organization manage its donation process.

Manage Donor Information

You should be able to store your donation and donor information automatically from the donation forms. In addition to securing donor information, encourage online donations by providing facts about the convenience of giving online. Share information concerning how you prevent online hacking and fraud to assure your donors that you value their security.

Accept Feedback

Create a space that allows your supporters to give you their feedback with regard to your operations. Then, consider using the feedback to improve your donation process. For example, a donor might request that the donation processing system automatically generate donation receipts and allow them to print. Another donor might suggest that you include their preferred payment option. Furthermore, you can receive positive reviews that can motivate your team and supporters.

Drive Donations

You can use strategies such as embedding a fundraising meter on your donation page for each campaign to increase donations. Fundraising meters show your visitors the progress of your campaign. Your audience can also automatically view the impact of their donation on the campaign by assessing the fundraising meter. This is more likely to encourage them to donate more so that the goal can be accomplished earlier.

SOCIAL MEDIA TIPS

Social media is an online interaction and networking platform that allows people to communicate by creating and sharing information. Examples of social media platforms include Facebook, Twitter, LinkedIn, Instagram, Snapchat, TikTok, and YouTube. Here are some of the best practices that can improve the experience of your social media followers when they visit your website.

- Sign up as a nonprofit - Social media platforms such as Facebook, YouTube, and Instagram offer features and resources that are devoted to only benefit nonprofits. These features include the ability to carry out fundraisers, promote your organization, as well as accept donations by adding donate buttons on your accounts. You can also connect your social media accounts to your website, email signature, and newsletter by adding their link addresses. Signing up as a nonprofit also exposes you to free online training opportunities designed to improve online operations for nonprofits. This includes learning how to activate your fundraising tools and donate buttons that allow other people to initiate fundraisers on behalf of your organization.

- Develop your social media guidelines - Provide your audience with clear guidelines on what to and not to post. It also outlines your security protocols to prevent hacking. Moreover, instructions ensure that you have relevant copyrights and know how to communicate or respond to negative feedback. Also, consider constructing a calendar that specifies what and when to post certain content on your accounts to remain active and consistent.

- Know your social media strategies - Pictures or videos of people acting toward solving a problem tend to gain more likes, views, and comments. However, you should avoid plagiarizing other people's images by acquiring appropriate permission from anyone featured in the graphics. Create hashtag campaigns to raise awareness. Hashtags are used to highlight important issues in simple and catchy phrases. Furthermore, your content should drive people to share with their peers. People tend to share content such as visuals, call to actions, motivational quotes, and informative facts.

Another way of increasing traffic to your accounts is by partnering with like-minded nonprofits, foundations, or individuals. This exposes you to new audiences. Not only can you promote campaigns on social media, but you can also host cheaper virtual events that can involve more people.

NEXT STEPS

In this chapter, we emphasized that your organization can use any social media platform to reach a broad audience cost-effectively. Social media also allows your organization to host virtual events, raise awareness, and drive change on a global scale. Your organization can benefit from an online presence by creating a superior website with good-quality content and design. Generally, your social media accounts should be accessible, user-friendly, secure, and trendy. You can increase your online revenues by smoothing your donation process. This includes generating simple donation forms, offering various online payment methods, and frequently updating your website. You should be exempt from paying tax on the donations that you receive. This aspect of tax exemption will be addressed in the next chapter.

APPLYING FOR TAX EXEMPTION

The main focus of this chapter is to provide information on how to complete the federal tax-exempt application in the United States. Information specific to countries discussed in Chapter 1, Australia, Canada, Ireland, and the United Kingdom, is found in the appendices. If you have completed the steps in previous chapters, then submitting the actual application will be relatively easy. We will also discuss an option of using fiscal sponsorship to enable fundraising while awaiting federal tax exemption and explain the procedures involved in different states.

FISCAL SPONSORSHIP

As there is a fee involved with applying for federal tax exemption and a waiting period for approval, some organizations choose to find a fiscal sponsor. Fiscal sponsorship is a partnership between a fledgling nonprofit and an established nonprofit. The existing nonprofit is already a tax-exempt entity and provides a new nonprofit with administrative, accounting, fundraising, and potentially legal services. Primarily, it enables new nonprofits to solicit public contributions that are tax deductible for the donor. In return, the fiscal sponsor receives anywhere from 5% to 15% of the funds collected on the new nonprofit's behalf.

These partnerships typically take the form of a comprehensive or pre-approved grant fiscal sponsorship. In a comprehensive fiscal sponsorship, the new nonprofit agrees to become a program of the fiscal sponsor. The sponsor is in charge both legally and monetarily and will own all the work products created by or for the projects, such as websites and fundraising materials. Your role would become a volunteer or employee working to support the project. Donations given to your project are treated as restricted funds for use to support your project only. This option does not preclude you from ever starting an official tax-exempt nonprofit, but can be used to gauge the idea's success. A comprehensive fiscal sponsorship can also help fund short-term projects like memorial contributions or recovery following a local disaster.

The second fiscal sponsorship option is a pre-approved grant relationship fiscal sponsorship. In this example, the project (your nonprofit idea) exists as a separate entity responsible for managing all aspects of the business. The project applies for a grant, which the fiscal sponsor funds from public contributions, foundations, or other funding sources. Contributions are tax-deductible because they are given to the fiscal sponsor. Ownership rights in the work product are negotiable and decided in a fiscal sponsor agreement.

Unfortunately, it is often difficult to find a sponsor with a similar charitable mission and vision, enough financial resources and knowledge to help get your project going, and willing to work with you. There is a national directory of organizations that serve as fiscal sponsors at https://fiscalsponsordirectory.org/. However, if you have followed this guide, you might find it is easier to form your own tax-exempt organization than to find a fiscal sponsor and complete its sponsorship application.

STATE INCORPORATION

Chapter 1 introduced the types of business structures available when starting a nonprofit. Here, we will expound on the registration procedures in different states. The organization must first be recognized as a business in the state you are operating in before applying for federal tax exemption. The process differs slightly in each state; however, the Secretary of State's website is usually the starting point for state incorporation.

Alabama

The first step that you should take for your nonprofit to be registered in Alabama is to form a corporation under the state's laws. From that stage, here are the next steps that you should follow:

- Choose at least three directors as you start your nonprofit.
- File a name reservation form to the Secretary of State. Upon following the instructions on the name reservation form, you can find out if the name you want is still available. When you then file your certificate of formation, attach the name reservation certificate with it.

- Hold the first board of directors meeting, which is often referred to as the "organization meeting of the board." The agenda of that meeting should include appointing officers, approving bylaws, and setting a tax year and accounting period. Make sure that there is a record of minutes for this meeting.
- Prepare your certificate of formation and file it with the Secretary of State for Alabama. You should pay a fee for your application to be processed, and this was $100 in 2020. Some of the information needed as you file your application includes the name and type of entity, purpose, duration, address, number of directors, and any other provisions meant to run the internal affairs of the nonprofit. You can find the certificate of formation form on the Alabama Secretary of State website, fill it out, and then submit it. *Please note that the state-provided certificate of formation contains the basic requirements for starting your nonprofit organization in Alabama. However, it does not include the language that the IRS requires for it to give you a 501(c)(3) federal tax exemption (refer to Chapter 5).
- Make sure your business license is in place.

- You might be required to register with the state before you can engage in any activities that are related to fundraising. You can get the forms for completing this registration from the Office of the Attorney General.
- When you receive a 501(c)(3) tax exemption from the IRS, you become an eligible candidate for exemption from income tax in Alabama. You can inquire with the Alabama Department of Revenue to find out more about how you can apply for other tax exemptions.

Alaska

Please note that the registration procedures for Alaska are similar to those for Alabama. However, in Alaska, you are required to file your articles of incorporation with the Corporations Section, Division of Corporations, Business, and Professional Licensing. You will also have to pay a filing fee, which was $50 in 2020.

All other procedures are the same as those that apply to Alabama. However, for more tax exemptions, make your inquiries with Alaska's Department of Revenue. Regulations with regard to registration requirements before fundraising are available on the Alaska Consumer Protection website.

Arizona

In Arizona, the filing fee for the Application to Reserve Limited Liability Company Name is $10 if you do it by mail. However, if you do it online, the overall cost is $45.

In addition to the steps that we mentioned for Alabama, nonprofits in Arizona are also expected to appoint a registered agent who will receive legal papers on their behalf. Please note that the agent that you choose is expected to have a street address in Arizona; a post office address is not accepted.

After filing the articles of association, nonprofit organizations in Arizona are also required to publish these documents at least three times in any newspaper in the county where the organization is located. The costs of these publications range from $60 to $200. Please note that if you are in Pima or Maricopa counties, the newspaper application rule does not apply. In Arizona, you will also have to file an annual report for a fee of $10 by postal mail or online.

With regard to registering before fundraising in the state, nonprofit organizations in Arizona are not required to do so.

Other States

The registration requirements for the following states are more or less the same as what we described for Alabama: Arkansas, Colorado, Connecticut, Delaware, D.C., Georgia, Hawaii, Idaho, Illinois, Kansas, Kentucky, Louisiana, Maine, Minnesota, Mississippi, North Carolina, North Dakota, Oklahoma, Oregon, Rhode Island, Tennessee, Utah, Vermont, Virginia, West Virginia, and Wisconsin.

For the following states, though there are many similarities with the registration and tax exemption requirements for Alabama, there are a few differences. Some of these requirements will be completed after you receive federal tax exemption. So, first, you incorporate in the state, then file Form 1023 or Form 1023-EZ, and, upon receipt of federal tax exemption, complete additional state forms to receive state tax exemption or approval to fundraise.

- **California**: You will need to file the FTB 3500A for you to be considered for state tax exemption. Remember, filing Form 1023 or Form 1023-EZ only provides federal tax exemption.
- **Florida**: You will need to get a registered agent to work with. To get an exemption from sales

tax, you should file another application with the Florida Department of Revenue. If you have more than three employees in your nonprofit organization, you will pay state reemployment taxes.

- **Iowa**: The nonprofit is not obliged to register with the state before it can carry out fundraising activities within the state.
- **Maryland**: You will still need to provide the following documents for exemption from state income tax: copies of bylaws, IRS tax determination letter, most recent financial statement, as well as an explanation of what your organization is all about.
- **Massachusetts:** You should fill in Form ST-2 and submit it to the Department of Revenue for you to be exempted from sales tax. For your nonprofit to be exempted from property taxes, you should complete an application that you will receive from your local assessor. Be sure to go through an online registration process with the Massachusetts Department of Revenue if you want your nonprofit to be exempted from income taxes. Keep your IRS 501(c)(3) determination copy at hand.
- **Michigan:** The IRS tax exemption for nonprofits comes with an automatic excuse

from use and sales taxes in Michigan. However, you should complete Form 3372 to claim this exemption, together with your IRS 501(c)(3) determination copy.

- **Missouri:** The 501(c)(3) determination letter from the IRS also comes with corporate tax exemption. To be exempted from use and sales taxes in Missouri, you should complete and submit Form 1746.

- **Montana:** Further registration with the state is not required before you can embark on fundraising activities.

- **Nebraska:** The 501(c)(3) tax exemption also applies to state corporate income tax.

- **Nevada:** This state has no corporate income tax, so you do not need to file any application for the exemption in this regard.

- **New Hampshire:** Please find out your state tax requirements from the New Hampshire Department of Revenue. You might have filing requirements that depend on your earnings.

- **New Jersey:** When your federal tax exemption has been approved by the IRS, complete Form REG-IE and submit it to the Exempt Organization Unit of the Division of Taxation.

- **New Mexico:** Exemption from the federal tax is accompanied by corporate income and franchise taxes exemption.

- **New York:** After you have been exempted from federal tax, file Form CT-247 with the New York Department of Taxation and Finance so that you can be exempted from corporate franchise taxes. Also, complete and file Form 25-119.2 with the New York State Department of Taxation and Finance so that you can get an exemption from sales taxes.

- **Ohio:** File Form STEC B with the Ohio Department of Taxation for your nonprofit organization to claim exemption from sales taxes.

- **Pennsylvania:** Federal tax exemption by the IRS comes with automatic corporate income tax exemption. However, you should file Form REV-72 with the Pennsylvania Department of Revenue so that your organization can be exempted from sales tax.

- **South Carolina:** You are automatically exempt from corporate income tax the moment the IRS gives you a 501(c)(3) tax-exempt status. For exemption from sales taxes, apply to the South Carolina Department of Revenue using Form

ST-387. For property tax exemption, file Form
PT-401-O with the Department of Revenue.

- **South Dakota:** This state does not have
  corporate taxes.
- **Texas:** After getting an exemption from federal
  tax, fill in and file Form AP-204 with the Texas
  Comptroller of Public Accounts as an
  application for exemption from the franchise,
  sales, and hotel taxes.
- **Washington:** This state has no corporate
  income tax.
- **Wyoming:** This state has no corporate taxes.

FEDERAL TAX-EXEMPTION

By now, you probably understand that the phrase "tax-
exempt" means that your nonprofit's income is not
subject to income tax. In this section, we will outline
the steps that you should take to attain tax-exempt
status, irrespective of the state where your organization
is operating.

If you want to file Form 1023, you will pay $600 to the
IRS. Filing the 1023-EZ comes with a fee of $275. It is
recommended that you file your tax-exempt application within 27 months after incorporation. This way,
your tax-exempt status will apply from the date your
organization was created. If you file your tax exemp-

tion after the 27-month period, your tax exemption will be applicable from the date you submit the application.

Form 1023 Versus Form 1023-EZ

There are two options when filing for federal tax exemption, both of which are submitted online through the pay.gov website. Form 1023 requires a lot of details, which you must precisely provide. Some of the pointers to what you should expect are your organization's history, structure, finances, operations, and governance policies.

If your organization is smaller, you can use Form 1023-EZ for your tax exemption application. This form is relatively simpler and shorter compared to Form 1023. For your nonprofit to qualify to use Form 1023-EZ, requirements include the following:

- The organization should be local, not foreign.
- The organization should not maintain donor-advised funds.
- The projected gross receipts should be below $50,000 in the next three years.
- The actual gross receipts should be below $50,000 for the past three years.
- The value of the organization's assets should be below $250,000.

- The nonprofit should not indicate interest in being classified as a private operating foundation or supporting organization.

The table below clarifies some of the differences between Form 1023 and Form 1023-EZ.

Form 1023	Form 1023-EZ
12 pages long	Three pages long
The presented questions require detailed responses.	Responses are via checkboxes.
You should provide bylaws, articles of incorporation, actual and projected financials, as well as the conflict of interest policy.	These may not be required.
A business plan that is consistent with 501(c)(3) is required.	There is no need for a business plan.
You will be contacted 180 days after submitting your application.	You will be contacted 90 days after submitting your application.

Please note that if you submit an EZ form and then end up having assets whose value exceeds $50,000, you are obliged to re-submit Form 1023 and will have to pay the higher fee. In addition, the IRS determination letter that you get after the approval shows that you used Form 1023-EZ to obtain the status. Potential donors who understand that the EZ form does not require a business plan, financial projections, or other incorporation documents may see your nonprofit organization as less authentic, which may negatively affect your organization's ability to attract donors.

Completing the Form

Given that you have followed the steps thus far outlined in the book, completing Form 1023 should be a simple and quick exercise. We will review the steps for Form 1023 versus Form 1023-EZ, as the latter is fairly self-explanatory. Both forms are submitted online at Pay.gov. Once you have created an account and logged in, enter Form 1023 in the search field. If you have chosen to submit Form 1023-EZ, select the search result for the Streamlined Application for Recognition of Exemption Under Section 501(c)(3). To continue with Form 1023, select the Application for Recognition of Exemption Under Section 501(c)(3) option. Detailed instructions for each step can be found at https://www.irs.gov/pub/irs-pdf/i1023.pdf; however, a high-level explanation of each part of the application with notes where applicable is included below.

Page 1 of 12, Part 1 - Identification of Applicant

In this section, you will enter your name and address, the organization's Employee Identification Number (EIN), the organization name and website address, and current board members' names and addresses.

Page 2 of 12, Part 2 - Organization Structure

On this page, you will identify the type of organization (for example, corporation, LLC, unincorporated association, or trust), date of incorporation, a state in which it was incorporated, and select that you have bylaws.

Page 3 of 12, Part 3 - Required Provisions in Organizing Document

As explained in Chapter 5, the Articles of Incorporation must include the following verbiage describing the organization's purpose:

The organization is organized exclusively for charitable, religious, educational, and scientific purposes under section 501(c)(3) of the Internal Revenue Code or corresponding section of any future federal tax code.

and dissolution:

Upon the dissolution of this organization, assets shall be distributed for one or more exempt purposes within the meaning of section 501(c)(3) of the Internal Revenue Code or corresponding section of any future federal tax code or shall be distributed to the federal government, or to a state or local government, for a public purpose.

You will need to find the page, article, and paragraph in the Articles of Incorporation in which these statements are included and enter them on this page of Form 1023.

Page 4 of 12, Part 4 - Activities

Section 4 requires you to explain the activities that the nonprofit organization will undertake. The instructions state not to repeat what is already written in the Articles of Incorporation. Rather, include an explanation for each past, present, and planned future activity that describes <u>what</u> the activity is and the total percentage of time and funds allocated to it, <u>who</u> will conduct it, <u>where</u> it will be conducted, <u>how</u> the activity furthers the exempt purpose and will be funded.

Page 5 of 12, Part 4 - Activities, continued

The continuation page of Part 4 requires you to answer a series of Yes/No questions regarding activities and select planned fundraising activities. It will also ask you to enter the appropriate 3-character NTEE Code that best describes your activities. It is recommended to select the checkbox that indicates you want the IRS to select the applicable NTEE Code.

Page 6 of 12, Part 5 - Compensation and Other Financial Arrangements

Answer a series of Yes/No questions in regard to whether board members receive compensation and whether there is a conflict of interest policy.

Page 7 of 12, Part 6 - Financial Data

Part 6 requires you to enter financial data, which you have already developed, as explained in Chapter 3. Include figures for the current year plus two additional years of revenues and expenses.

Page 8 of 12, Part 6 - Financial Data, continued

On the continuation page of Part 6, you will enter information from the Balance Sheet (that is, Assets and Liabilities) for your most recently completed tax year.

Page 9 of 12, Part 7 - Foundation Classification

The information provided in this book assumes you decided to apply for 5013c classification, in which case you would select the following option:

- You are a publicly supported organization and would like the IRS to decide your correct classification.

Descriptions of other options, such as the 509 classifications listed in this question, can be found on the IRS website. If the organization has been in existence for more than five years, you will also be required to answer a series of questions confirming your public support status.

Page 10 of 12, Part 8 - Effective Date

This section validates that the application submission is within 27 months of the end of the month in which you were legally formed. If this is not applicable to your situation, then you also have to complete Schedule E.

Page 11 of 12, Part 9 - Annual Filing Requirements

Answer No to being exempt from Filing Form 990.

Page 12 of 12, Part 10 - Signature

The last part is just to electronically sign your application. Before submitting, you will also want to assemble the document that includes all of your supporting documentation. It is recommended to include the organization's EIN in the header of the document. The document should be saved in .pdf format and be less than 15 MB. You can copy all files into one Microsoft Word or Google Docs file and then Print to PDF. Once saved, validate the file size. The following information should be included:

- Organizing documents and any amendments (for example, articles of incorporation, constitution, trust document, conflict of interest, and sexual harassment policies)
- Bylaws, if adopted

- Signed & completed Form 2848, Power of Attorney and Declaration of Representative (not applicable because you are submitting Form 1023 yourself)
- Signed & completed Form 8821, Tax Information Authorization, if applicable
- Supplemental responses, if applicable (for example, narrative description of activities and budget), and
- Expedited handling request, if applicable

The Letter of Determination

The letter of determination is a sign that your application for 501(c)(3) federal tax exemption has been approved. This achievement opens the door to the following advantages:

- You automatically get an exemption from federal income tax.
- The credibility of your organization's mission is authenticated.
- It becomes possible for donors to claim contributions on their annual tax returns.
- You qualify for grant funding applications for tax-exempt organizations.
- You can enjoy discounts on the rates for USPS postage.

NEXT STEPS

This chapter extensively explored the incorporation process for different states within the United States. We also looked at the federal tax exemption forms (Form 1023 and Form 1023-EZ) and compared the documents and fees required for each, as well as the timeframes involved. The next chapter is an information reservoir on keeping appropriate business records.

8

KEEPING RECORDS

R
ecord keeping can be a nightmare when you are unsure of what you are supposed to do. This is why we compiled this chapter to enlighten you on the correct methods for keeping records in your nonprofit. We will begin by looking at the importance of proper record-keeping before delving into the nitty-gritty of the procedures involved.

WHY IT IS IMPORTANT

One of the common reasons why nonprofit organizations keep records is to comply with legal requirements. There is no stipulated method for record-keeping, according to the law. Every nonprofit does it in a way that suits its activities and mission. However, whichever way you choose to keep records in your organization, many other benefits come with the effort, apart from compliance with tax requirements and other law-related reasons. Let's look at some of the pros of up-to-date record keeping.

Monitoring Programs

You will engage in various activities and programs to further your primary goals as an organization. These programs should be monitored, which can be done via excellent record-keeping. Keeping proper records helps to monitor the progress of the programs to see if desired results are being obtained. Record keeping may also assist in identifying areas of improvement for current and future programs. Moreover, keeping records for ongoing programs may contribute to success as the people involved know they are being monitored.

Tracking Receipts

With good record-keeping strategies, you can easily identify the sources of various receipts, no matter how many. This also helps to clarify program receipts from the non-program ones. Receipts also assist in separating taxable and nontaxable income. Finally, you can also use them to assess how much you receive from your fundraising activities.

Preparing Tax Returns

Any flow of finances should be highlighted on tax returns. The financial records of your nonprofit are also monitored and inspected by the government, so they should be up-to-date. When record keeping is done well, preparing the assessments that the government requires takes less time. You should keep records of the income and expenditure to clarify the nonprofit's revenues. Such financial information will be helpful when working with funding organizations, creditors, and banks.

RECORD-KEEPING BASICS

You might have heard of the adage that says, "If it's not in writing, it didn't happen." Unfortunately, this cannot be said any better because good record-keeping is one of the basic units for transparency and the success of your organization. However, the critical question is, "What records do you have to keep to have a basic but good track of your records?" The answer to this crucial question will be given in this section, which will take you through the basics that form the foundation of record keeping. We will focus on accounting, contributions, and corporate and activity records to get that done.

Accounting

Your financial records should be on point as you practice Generally Accepted Accounting Principles (GAAP). When it comes to your financial reports, you should emphasize completeness, accuracy, and consistency. One of the major things that many nonprofit organizations need to improve is procrastination, which often negatively affects aspects such as accuracy and consistency. Unfortunately, preparing tax documents is challenging when accounts need to be fixed. If you see that no one within your organization is an "accounts person," these services are worth hiring into your nonprofit.

Donations

Records of what has been given to your organization are vital, along with the amounts and people behind the funding. Please note that cash and in-kind donations should be recorded accurately and timely. This information is essential when you prepare your tax forms. For example, when a nonprofit in the United States completes Form 990, all donors whose donations are at least $5,000 must be listed on Schedule B of Form 990 or Form 990-EZ. In some cases, nonprofits must list all donors who would have given them at least 2% of the total donated revenue.

Apart from being used for tax reasons, information about donations is also crucial for tracking the data for donors, especially in light of enhancing accuracy when calculating the public support test. Moreover, keeping track of information about consistent donors is an excellent strategy for looking after the financial health of your organization.

Corporate Records

Some of the more obvious corporate documents include bylaws, articles of incorporation, and annual reports. However, it is easier to forget the minutes of the board meetings that were held. Minutes are records of all the proceedings in board meetings, as well as the decisions that were made. These are some of the records that government agencies might look for in their evaluations. Besides, keeping such records explains some actions taken in the organization. For instance, if you compensate the director of the nonprofit, there has to be some documentation that shows how this was done. Minutes also come in handy in the event of legal disputes; they might save the day!

Activity Records

In this category of record keeping, all activities that your organization engaged in should be mentioned. This includes fundraising, and in this case, you have to be clear on how the activity was done and the proceeds that were accumulated. You should also highlight the overall costs of planning and carrying out the fundraising program. Questions like "How many people benefited from the activity or program?" should also be answered in your records. Even the littlest detail is vital, considering that the government also assesses fundraising activities. Moreover, information such as this can even increase your donor base as people see transparency in procedures, proceedings, and outcomes. Documentation also helps to finetune the delivery of future activities, as you can review what went well and what can be improved upon.

DOCUMENT RETENTION POLICIES

As you start your nonprofit organization, the documents you generate may be kept for years because the information might still be reasonable. Imagine a situation where you have piles of various papers that might become more of a mess than a way of being organized. In that case, you should develop a document retention policy that helps you manage the records.

Generally, you should identify the documents that must stick around for longer. This should be stipulated in the document retention policy. There should be a schedule that allows for the regular destruction of documents that the organization will no longer need. Some tax forms also require information on whether the nonprofit organization has a written document retention policy in place.

What Should You Retain?

There is no overall template that highlights the documents that should be retained. This is because of the vast differences in the organizations' activities. So, at the end of the day, the documents tagged as "important" differ for each nonprofit. Moreover, state and province regulations that govern nonprofit organizations also vary. Therefore, organizations should retain documents that are required by local regulations. However, there are a few documents that nearly all nonprofits should keep for as long as they exist. These include the following:

- checks
- insurance policy
- tax returns
- corporate resolutions
- minutes from meetings
- annual financial statements
- mortgages, real estate deeds, and bills of sale
- articles of incorporation

- nonprofit, tax-exempt determination letters
  and any related correspondences
- audit reports

Be sure to check with your local association of
nonprofits in case they have a sample document retention policy specific to your region. In addition, they
might provide free resources to their members.

Quick Pointers

How best can you practice document retention? Here
are some pointers:

- If there are documents that you are keeping
  digitally, remember to back them up.
- Consider documents you could retain for
  history or memory purposes and keep them for
  longer or permanently.
- Be sure to check state and province laws
  associated with employment, considering that
  they often vary. These laws do affect your
  document retention policy.
- You can also adopt the suggestions of the
  professional handling your accounts, as they
  may have a better idea of the documents that
  might be required in the event of an audit.

- Adding a preamble to your policy might be a great idea. This may help to bring out the link between the policy and the board's fiduciary role.

HELPFUL SOFTWARE

Keeping things organized is the best way to enhance success, even from a time-related perspective, as you can find what you are looking for more easily. QuickBooks is a tool that helps you organize various aspects of finance, including expenses and donations. The interface for QuickBooks is user-friendly, so you will not waste time learning how to navigate the software that would otherwise be directed to the organization's primary mission. QuickBooks provides the following features.

- **Accounting software:** Nonprofit finances need to be closely monitored, which requires effective software. This is where QuickBooks comes in; you may have to leave your old spreadsheets.
- **Reporting:** Reporting is much easier with QuickBooks as it has more than 200 built-in reports you can customize. You can even create

your own templates, thereby creating reports that keep all relevant stakeholders informed.

- **Tracking grants and donations:** With QuickBooks, you won't only edit the profiles of the donors, but you can also track their trends in supporting your organization. You also use the software to customize reports that you can use in outreaches. It is also possible for QuickBooks to integrate with plugins, payment processors, donor pages, and software for donor management. This makes it easier for you to manage donations, gifts, and expenses from one place.

- **Automation of the accounting:** Some features in QuickBooks are automated. These include recurring payrolls, workflows, invoicers, and data analysis. Such automated features leave no room for mistakes, which makes your accounting better, quicker, and more efficient.

QuickBooks and Other Nonprofit Software

QuickBooks has many supported integrations, a property that makes it possible for this tool to bring together accounting data in one place. The ability of QuickBooks to track expenses, pay your bills, trace donor patterns, and manage payroll and fundraising programs is aided by the various apps that are integrated into this software. Nonprofit CRM and donor management software that integrates well with QuickBooks is available. One good one is Kindful integration, which enhances tasks such as financial reporting, real-time updates, and contacts management.

Alternatives to QuickBooks

QuickBooks is a great option when it comes to accounting for nonprofit organizations. However, there are other alternatives that you can consider. Here are good examples, all of which are free:

- **Nonprofit Treasurer:** This tool is best for smaller nonprofits. It helps with reporting, budgeting, and general financial accounting.
- **MoneyMinder:** Some features you will find on MoneyMinder are budgeting templates and a document library. This program allows you to reconcile bank accounts and follow up on volunteer programs. You can even send receipts of acknowledgment to your organization's donors.
- **Adminsoft Accounts:** With this software, you have access to a double-entry accounting system. Payroll management is also possible.
- **Wave Accounting:** Wave Accounting is an online tool that makes accounting and

invoicing easier. Other functionalities found on this program are payroll and finance management, processing credit cards, and tracking payments.

- **FrontAccounting ERP:** This program allows you to manage reports, ledgers, and bank accounts. It has multiple-user access functionality.

CORPORATE BINDER

A corporate binder is where you will keep the hard copies of the records pertaining to your nonprofit organization. It can be as simple as a three-ring binder from an office supply store with index dividers. Alternatively, you can purchase a corporate kit with a binder and tabs, a corporate seal, and membership certificates (if applicable). Be sure to clearly label the binder with the name of your nonprofit organization. In addition to records of meeting proceedings, your nonprofit's corporate binder should also include the following:

- Articles of incorporation
- Bylaws
- Board member names and contact information
- Applicable business permits and licenses

NONPROFIT STARTUP GUIDE | 173

- Tax exemption approval letter
- Insurance coverage details
- Employee and volunteer policies

NEXT STEPS

The information that we discussed in this chapter increases your record-keeping acumen. Implementing the nuggets that you learned is more likely to make record management much easier than you thought. Both online and physical record-keeping methods have been explained, as have the necessary tools. With all the information you have acquired, you might ask, "Now what?" Get your answer in the next chapter, where we explore the next steps.

9

NEXT STEPS

Now that your nonprofit organization is legally established, you should put strategies in place that allow you to attract as many donors as possible. You can do that by allowing your organization to be evaluated. How you can do this is explained in this chapter. The chapter also reviews additional steps to position your nonprofit for growth, such as opening a bank account and obtaining necessary insurance.

OPENING A BANK ACCOUNT

Opening a bank account for your nonprofit is a relatively straightforward process. However, the exact time to complete this step in the nonprofit startup process can vary. You need a bank account to connect to your donation processing software (e.g., PayPal, GiveLify). However, banks that may provide free accounts for approved nonprofit status will require documentation. So, you might wait to set up the account once you have your official exempt status from the government.

Before selecting your banking institution, conduct research on available options. Some local banks might be more likely to provide assistance or sponsor an event for your nonprofit. You can also ask potential banks what their experience is working with nonprofits. Having an expert in nonprofit funding options such as tax-exempt loans, bonds, and financing could be valuable.

To open an account, you generally need to make sure you have the tax ID number, bylaws, incorporation documents, and the exemption letter. You are also required to have the identification of your treasurer and the officers who sign checks for your organization.

OBTAINING INSURANCE

In most cases, nonprofit organizations operate on limited budgets, which is partly why they should have insurance. However, choosing the appropriate insurance for your nonprofit is essential. Let's discuss the choices that you have.

Liability Insurance

General liability insurance, also called commercial general liability or CGL, protects the nonprofit if someone is injured on the organization's premises. Please note that the GCL is not applicable to the nonprofit's employees.

Professional liability insurance, also known as "malpractice" or "errors and omissions" insurance, protects employees, directors, officers, volunteers, and the entire organization from liabilities that may arise from various forms of organizational mismanagement. It also covers claims such as sexual harassment and discrimination.

Product liability insurance should be acquired by nonprofits that sell goods to the public as a way of raising funds. This type of insurance will come in handy if, say, the buyers complain that the sold products hurt them or were defective.

Auto Insurance

Auto liability insurance applies when volunteers or staff members use their personal vehicles to complete the nonprofit's tasks. Depending on the rules that apply in your state or province, you may need to buy a minimum amount of coverage. This way, the insurance will compensate if the driver injures others or property while on duty. In some cases, the nonprofit may be required to purchase coverage for personal injury protection (PIP) and uninsured/underinsured motorist (UM/UIM) coverage.

Directors and Officers Insurance

Unlike professional liability insurance, which also includes other stakeholders in the organization, directors and officers insurance (commonly referred to as D&O) only covers directors and officers and their spouses. Suppose the directors or officers of your nonprofit are individually named in a lawsuit due to allegations of, say, financial management. In that case, D&O insurance protects the personal assets of the directors and officers and typically covers legal fees and settlements. Please note that criminal behavior is not covered.

Property Insurance

Property insurance protects the organization's assets, like the space from which it operates. This insurance may also cover furniture, computers and accessories, fixtures such as carpets, equipment, and machinery, as well as inventory and supplies.

OBTAINING A CHARITY RATING

Australia

In Australia, ChangePath helps provide the public with information they need to give to charity organizations. They aid in the transparency that, when absent, makes potential donors hesitate to fund nonprofits.

Creating an account on ChangePath can be done by anyone, though editing company information is limited to direct employees. If you want the benefit of immediately accessing your organization's profile, consider using the email address associated with your nonprofit. Once access has been granted, you will be required to prove that you are a direct employee of the nonprofit. You may need to provide your government-issued ID and a proof of employment letter to do this. Be ready to provide any additional information if requested by the ChangePath team. Once you are given access to editing the information on your organization's profile, you can add new information, make edits to basic information, and add projected outcomes. For edits on core information, you should make a request first.

Ratings are based on three main components—transparency, finances, and outcomes. How the rating is done is different for each component. After the ratings, you will receive badges for each component, depending on the results.

Canada

In Canada, Charity Intelligence provides donors with a summary of information about the charities they might be interested in. These details are provided in the form of a rating that ranges from zero to five. Generally, the overall rating is determined by evaluating these components:

- Results reporting (35%)
- Impact (20%)
- Room for funding (15%)
- Financial transparency (15%)
- Cost-efficiency (15%)

For your nonprofit organization to qualify for a four- or five-star rating, the table below provides a guide for which to aim.

Evaluated component	Five-star rating	Four-star rating
Cost ratio for fundraising	Less than 30%	Less than 42%
Cost coverage for the program	Less than 300%	Less than 500%
Cost ratio for administration	Below 30%	Below 35%
Financial transparency	Two and above rating	Two and above rating
Results reporting	Within upper 50% of charities	Within upper 60% of charities

Ireland

In Ireland, the Charity Regulator monitors nonprofits, ensuring that they comply with the Charities Act. The Charity Regulator publishes information about nonprofits, which can be accessed and used by potential donors. In enhancing its roles, the Charity Regulator upholds the following values:

- Independence: The Charity Regulator makes its decisions as an independent entity but with the public interest in mind.
- Accountability: The made decisions are based on evidence. Therefore, they are confident of the information that they release to the sector, and so they take full responsibility for their actions.

- Fairness: The Charity Regulator upholds impartiality and consistency in their procedures and decision-making processes.
- Proportionality: They recognize and appreciate the fact that the organizations that they regulate are diverse, hence the need to implement proportionate measures that accommodate everyone.
- Respect: They take a respectful, collaborative, and accommodating approach when dealing with all stakeholders.

United Kingdom

In the United Kingdom, Charity Clarity provides as much information as possible to potential donors so that they can make informed decisions. Charity Clarity's inclusion criteria for nonprofits to assess are as follows:

- Location: Charity Clarity only assesses organizations that are located in the United Kingdom.
- Legal standing: Charities are considered if they are registered with the UK's Charity Commission.
- Evidence-based length of operations: The organization should provide accounts that span

at least two or preferably more years.

Learn more about possible ratings from Charity Clarity in the table below.

Rating	Meaning	Explanation
1	Poor	Performance is way below average and the organization is outperformed by almost all charities.
2	Requires improvement	Doesn't meet standards and is outperformed by most charities.
3	Average	Close to meeting standards, and its performance is similar to that of many charities.
4	Good	Is on par with most standards, and the performance is better than that of most charities.
5	Excellent	Excels beyond the standards set while outperforming most charities.

United States

Let's explore how you can enhance your visibility to donors in the United States.

Guidestar

Customizing your organization's profile is an excellent way to make it attractive to potential donors. You can even decide what information you want tens of millions of donors to see about your nonprofit. To get started, you should claim a profile of your nonprofit organization, and the first step in doing so is creating a personal account on Guidestar, which is now under the Candid umbrella. Remember to use your organization's email address so that you get immediate access.

Please note that if you have recently received your federal tax exemption (that is, within the last six months), you can manually create your profile by uploading a copy of the federal determination letter; however, organizations manually listed on GuideStar will not be verified until they appear on the IRS Business Master File (BMF). You cannot apply to be a recognized charity with Facebook until the IRS Business Master File has been updated with your tax-exempt status.

Charity Navigator

The Charity Navigator evaluates nonprofits on a scale from zero to four. Potential donors use such ratings to determine the authenticity and success of various nonprofit organizations. Please note that only 501(c)(3) tax-exempt organizations are rated. To earn your organization's rating, log in to the "Charity Navigator Nonprofit Portal" and provide the required information by following the prompts.

The table below shows the ratings that are found on the Charity Navigator.

Rating	Evaluation	More information
0	Great	Meets or exceeds the standards in most areas.
1	Good	Meets or exceeds the standards in some areas.
2	Requires improvement	Meets or nearly meets in a few areas but underperforms many charities.
3	Poor	Doesn't meet standards in most areas and underperforms virtually all charities.
4	Very poor	Performance is below industry-stipulated standards.

You might be wondering how your organization is rated; the criteria are as follows:

- Impact and results (50%)
- Accountability and finance (32.5%)
- Culture and community (10%)
- Leadership and adaptability (7.5%)

GiveWell

GiveWell identifies nonprofits that are excelling in their performance so that they can give donors insights on which organizations to support. GiveWell assesses organizations based on the cost-effectiveness of their programs, transparency, effectiveness, and an identifiable need for more funding. The process that is used in coming up with the final evaluations follows these steps:

- identifying organizations that are eligible
- examining the selected nonprofit organizations
- following up on the organization to further assess their progress and performance

NEXT STEPS

In this chapter, we have explored how evaluations for nonprofits are done. With the nuggets you've gained, you can work hard so that your organization shines as brightly as the highly rated ones and gains the visibility you need to attract donors.

Congratulations on making it to the end of this book. With the wealth of information you have learned, you can confidently start your nonprofit organization. Now it is time to implement what you learned and live your dream of meeting specific community needs.

HELP ANOTHER NON-PROFIT GET OFF THE GROUND

I'm sure you're eager to get started, but before you do, I'd like to ask you to take a moment to help someone else in the same position.

Simply by sharing your honest opinion of this book on Amazon, you'll show new readers where they can find all the information they need to get their own non-profit organization off the ground.

LEAVE A REVIEW!

Thank you for your support... Together, we can make the world a better place.

CONCLUSION

The Nonprofit Startup Guide has taken you through the journey of starting your own nonprofit organization. This book kicked off by exploring various classifications for nonprofit organizations. This was meant to help you start on the right footing as you choose the classification that works best for your goals. Once you are sure of your preferred and appropriate classification, you should create a strategic plan that maps your way forward. You then have to develop mission and vision statements that clearly reflect what your organization is all about.

Another important aspect of creating a nonprofit is developing a realistic and detailed budget. A reasonable budget informs your decisions with regard to fundraising strategies. With a clear budget, even donors will know the financial needs of your organization. Creating your organization's budget is spearheaded by the board of directors, so your nonprofit should have one. Requirements on the number of members that should make up a board vary with countries or states, but usually, the board is comprised of at least three people.

The legal existence of your nonprofit depends on the availability of relevant documents. These documents include the articles of incorporation and bylaws, for which a basic outline was provided. In addition, as a nonprofit organization, you are entitled to tax exemptions. We took you through the process of applying for tax exemption, a step that will assist you in saving funds and directing them toward enhancing your vision and mission.

For your organization to be well-recognized and make a reasonable impact, you should establish an online presence. You can do this by creating a website or taking advantage of social media. A guide for creating a good website has been highlighted in this book. Another vital aspect that we emphasized in this book was record keeping. Be sure to put together effective strategies for keeping important documents, donor information, and financial data. This kind of management is essential to the success of your organization.

Creating a nonprofit organization entails a lot of paperwork and documents, but with this guidebook in hand, you'll find that registration is not that difficult at all. Your dream social startup is within your grasp. Good luck!

If you have found this book useful, please leave a review to help another person who has a similar passion to yours.

APPENDIX A: UNITED STATES 501 (C) NONPROFIT DESIGNATIONS

- **501(c)(1):** Nonprofits that fall under this category are enhanced by Congress. Contributions can be collected only if they will be directed toward public benefit.
- **501(c)(2):** A nonprofit organization that is operated under another organization that is exempted from tax falls under the 501(c)(2) classification. Such organizations surrender all their proceeds to the parent organization under which they function.
- **501(c)(3):** You can refer to nonprofits in this class as "charitable organizations." Religious and literary organizations also fall under this category. Funding of such organizations is usually via donations, government grants, and membership dues.
- **501(c)(4):** These nonprofit organizations focus on supporting those who are going through difficult times by improving their welfare. Social welfare organizations fall under this

category. Social Advocacy Groups are also classified under 501(c)(4). Their sole purpose is to lobby for a specific cause, be it political or social.

- **501(c)(5):** Nonprofits that fall under this category should have a mission that is oriented toward agriculture and horticulture and the labor involved. Their services are meant to better the working atmosphere and improve educational capacity.
- **501(c)(6):** You can think of these as Trade or Professional Associations. Their aim is to make the working and operating conditions of their members better. Good examples include real estate boards and business leagues.
- **501(c)(7):** These nonprofit organizations are created to organize and run certain recreational activities. Sports clubs fall under this type of nonprofit.
- **501(c)(8):** This type of nonprofit comprises fraternal societies. Their existence is hinged upon covering expenses that are related to sickness, accidents, and death.
- **501(c)(9):** Picture this as the Employee Beneficiary Association. They offer financial assistance to members who would have

encountered traumatic events, including sickness.

- **501(c)(10):** These are Domestic Fraternal Societies and Associations that offer financial support for outside causes without directly making payments to members. The money that is used for this noble cause is taken from membership dues.
- **501(c)(11):** These nonprofits are driven to organize funds for teachers' retirements. They are commonly known as the Teachers' Retirement Fund Association.
- **501(c)(13):** The purpose of these nonprofits is to take part in burial proceedings for their members. This is why they are also referred to as cemetery companies.
- **501(c)(14):** These organizations, also known as the State Chartered Credit Union and Mutual Reserve Fund, provide their members with financial services, with discounts. Their sources of income are government grants and business activities.
- **501(c)(15):** You can call these nonprofits "Mutual Insurance Companies of Association." The members pay certain fees in exchange for insurance coverage against funerals and property damage.

- **501(c)(16):** These are Cooperative Organizations to Finance Crop Operations. They are made up of farmers who agree to combine their agricultural resources to enhance agricultural operations.
- **501(c)(17):** These nonprofits depend on the support of employers and/or employees in a bid to assist those who are permanently unemployed or those who are on sick leave. If you have ever heard of the Supplemental Unemployment Benefits Trust, then these are the 501(c)(17) nonprofit organizations.
- **501(c)(18):** These nonprofits are classified under the Employee Funded Pension Trust. In this case, members of employee trusts contribute money that is then used for payments.
- **501(c)(19):** Think of these as Veteran Organizations, where at least 75% of the members should be active or retired members of the army. The services of such nonprofit organizations are enjoyed by members of the U.S. armed forces.
- **501(c)(21):** This type is also referred to as the Black Lung Benefits Trust. Their services are based on the Federal Black Lung Benefits Act of

1969. They offer assistance to coal miners who are victims of black lung disease.

- **501(c)(22):** This type is funded by employers so that they can meet their obligations for pension payments. It is generally known as the Withdrawal Liability Payment Fund.
- **501(c)(23):** This type of nonprofit is applicable to veterans organizations that were established prior to 1884.
- **501(c)(26):** These are State Sponsored Organizations Providing Health Coverage for High-Risk Individuals. The aim of such nonprofits is to enhance access to proper healthcare for high-risk individuals who may not have the capacity to get it.
- **501(c)(27):** This type is also referred to as the State Sponsored Workers' Compensation Reinsurance Organization. These nonprofits ensure workers' compensation programs. Their sources of funds are members' dues and government grants.

APPENDIX B: AUSTRALIA CONSIDERATIONS

CREATING ARTICLES OF INCORPORATION

In Australia, there are various ways in which you can register your nonprofit organization. These different routes of registration depend on the purpose of your organization, which further determines the structure that works best for you. Basically, you can register your organization as a company or an incorporated association.

As a Company

In this case, your organization will be registered as a public company that is limited by guarantee. This means that the members of the company have limited liability. Another point to note is that if your organization is registered this way, then it becomes a separate legal entity from the members. The implication of this effect is that your organization can be sued in its own capacity.

For your organization to be registered as a company, the list below shows some of the considerations that are made. The company is expected to

- consist of at least one secretary and three directors.
- have an office that is registered and actively used for its purposes in Australia.
- have a governing constitution.
- keep clear and up-to-date financial records.
- keep a record of its members' register.

As an Incorporated Association

Just like the company set-up, a company that is registered as an incorporated association also operates as a separate legal entity. Registration of these associations is not administered by the Australian Securities and Investments Commission (ASIC) but is done under territory or state regulation. This means that you can only conduct your operations in the area where your organization is registered unless you file an application to become a registrable Australian body.

If your organization is registered as an incorporated association, you will be required to

- have a public officer.
- be governed by legislation rules.
- set up a committee that is responsible for the management of the organization.
- have a registered office.
- have clear financial records.
- maintain registers for all members, including those on the committee.

APPLYING FOR A REGISTRATION NUMBER

You will need to get an Australian Business Number (ABN):

- for tax obligation registration
- so that you can be endorsed as a deductible gift receiver (DGR)
- to be endorsed as a registered charity

When you apply for an ABN, make sure you know your organization's type and entity as this information will be required. If you provide the wrong information, you might need to repeat the application process. You can file your application online via the Australian Business Register. You will also need to set up myGovID and Relationship Authorisation Manager (RAM) so that you can access various online services on behalf of your nonprofit.

OBTAINING TAX EXEMPTION IN AUSTRALIA

You can make a self-assessment to see if your organization can be exempt from tax. This assessment should be done on an annual analysis to determine if your organization is still eligible for tax exemption. Here are the steps that you can follow in doing this evaluation:

1. Identify if your organization can be categorized as a charity.
2. If the answer to (1) above is a resounding yes, then check if you are registered with the Australian Charities and Not-for-profits Commission (ACNC).
3. If the answer to (2) above is yes, then the organization needs to be endorsed by the Australian Taxation Office (ATO) so that it can be exempted from income tax.

OBTAINING TAX EXEMPTION IN THE UNITED STATES

From the United States' perspective, foreign organizations are those that were created in countries other than the United States, its territories, or its possessions. Foreign organizations may apply for tax-exempt status on income earned in the United States in the same way that domestic organizations apply for exempt status (see Chapter 7 for details). Keep in mind that contributions by U.S. residents to foreign organizations generally are not deductible.

A foreign organization that obtains exemption as a public charity must file an information return annually (Form 990 or Form 990-EZ). A foreign organization that is a private foundation must file Form 990-PF annually. However, a foreign organization, other than a private foundation or a section 509(a)(3) supporting organization, may file Form 990-N (e-Postcard) instead of Form 990 or Form 990-EZ when its gross receipts from TIP U.S. sources are normally $50,000 or less and it has not conducted significant activity in the United States.

APPENDIX C: CANADA CONSIDERATIONS

CREATING ARTICLES OF INCORPORATION

Incorporation of organizations is done under federal, provincial, or territorial statutes in Canada. These statutes determine the documents that are required for nonprofit organizations to register for incorporation. Despite the statutes, make sure you use certified governing documents, not draft ones. Otherwise, you risk having your application returned because it will be considered incomplete. Also, be sure to indicate that your organization's services are for the benefit of the public.

If your organization is registered under the federal statute, it can use its registered name in any province or territory in Canada. However, it still has to observe any territorial or provincial stipulations. If your nonprofit is registered under provincial or territorial statutes, it can use its registered name in the respective territory or province. Please, take note that the incorporation guidelines in some provinces can cause problems when you are applying for registration with the Canada Revenue Agency (CRA).

APPLYING FOR A REGISTRATION NUMBER

In Canada, it is possible to get your business number (BN) via business registration online (BRO). Once you have your BN, you qualify to apply to register for the following program accounts:

- payroll discounts
- information returns
- corporation income tax
- Import-export

OBTAINING TAX EXEMPTION IN CANADA

To apply for qualified donee status in Canada, follow these steps:

- Set up your nonprofit organization. Prepare governing documents and clearly state the purpose of your organization.
- File your application for registration. To do this, first, create a list of the required documents and make sure they are all available. Describe all the charitable activities that are

associated with your organization. Submit your application online.

- Wait for the outcome after your application has been reviewed. If you submit an incomplete application, it will be returned. However, you will receive a letter of acknowledgment if your application is complete. During the review process, you might be asked to clarify some issues and this should be done within 60 days. Please note that your application's outcome may come out as rejected or approved. If your application is denied, you are allowed to submit a notice of objection to appeal against the outcome.

OBTAINING TAX EXEMPTION IN THE UNITED STATES

Canadian organizations that have received a Notification of Registration from the Canada Revenue Agency (formerly Canada Customs and Revenue Agency), and whose registrations have not been revoked, are automatically recognized in the United States as section 501(c)(3) organizations and are not required to file Form 1023.

Canadian registered charities are also presumed to be private foundations. If you are a Canadian registered charity and want to be listed as a section 501(c)(3) organization on IRS.gov or request classification as a public charity rather than a private foundation, gather the following information and mail or fax to:

Internal Revenue Service Exempt Organization Determinations - Room 6403

P.O. Box 2508

Cincinnati, OH 45201

- A letter stating the organization's request (listing as a section 501(c)(3) organization on IRS.gov or classification as a public charity).
- The legal name and complete mailing address of the organization.
- The organization's EIN.
- The month its tax year ends.
- The organization's date of formation.
- A contact name and telephone number.
- The public charity status it is requesting (if applicable) and information demonstrating how it meets the requirements of that status.
- This penalty of perjury statement:

I declare under the penalties of perjury that I have examined this request, including the accompanying documents, and to the best of my knowledge and belief, the request contains all the relevant facts relating to the request, and such facts are true, correct, and complete.

- The signature of an officer, director, trustee, or other authorized person.
- A copy of the organization's Notification of Registration.
- Form 8833, Treaty-Based Return Position Disclosure Under Section 6114 or 7701(b)

APPENDIX D: IRELAND CONSIDERATIONS

CREATING ARTICLES OF INCORPORATION

As introduced in Chapter 1, there are three ways that nonprofits can be legally structured in Ireland: as an unincorporated association, a trust, or a company limited by guarantee. Charities operating as trusts require a governing document called a trust deed, which explains the objectives of the trust, and the appointment, power and removal of trustees.

For charity organizations that operate as unincorporated associations, the Charities Regulator stipulates that they should have a written constitution. This written agreement should comprise the following:

- the association's name
- the aims and objectives
- information about people who are governing the association
- the Trustees' roles and contractual agreement
- property and income clauses

The main documents that govern the companies limited by guarantees (CLGs) are the articles of association and the memorandum. Some of the aspects that are covered in the articles of association are

- the organization's name.
- the charitable activities that it does.
- the company's members.
- general meetings.
- the appointment, roles, and removal of the board of directors.
- directors' meetings.
- minutes for meetings.
- audits and accounts.
- policies that govern all the operations of the organization.
- the powers that are vested in the nonprofit, as well as the boundaries that should be observed.
- the use of property and income; these should be used to further the organization's goals to serve the public.

The property and income statement is crucial in order for a nonprofit organization to obtain tax exemption as a charity. This clause must state that all income and property of the organization are to be applied solely toward its charitable main objects. The Revenue

Commissioners also require that donations should be at arm's-length and the use of the funds is subject only to the charity's governing instrument.

Irish nonprofits can apply for the registration online or physically. Once your application has been approved, you will receive a certificate of incorporation from the Companies Registration Office. Generally, it should take about 15 days for your company to be registered if all requirements are met. It is even quicker when you use the model governing document for filing your application.

APPLYING FOR A REGISTRATION NUMBER

Registered nonprofit organizations attain a Registered Charity Number (RCN). If you have a charitable tax exemption, you will also obtain a charity reference number, which is often known as the "CHY number."

OBTAINING TAX EXEMPTION IN IRELAND

The first requirement for registering for tax exemption is being granted charitable status by the Charities Regulatory Authority (CRA). You should also be registered for tax with Revenue, and this is done by completing Form TR1 if you are an incorporated body, Form TR2 if you are a company, or the Tax

Registration form if you are a nonprofit organization. Also, you have to register for Revenue Online Services (ROS).

Submit your application for tax exemption via ROS. To do this, sign it to ROS, prior to clicking "My Services," and then go to "Other Services." Choose "Charities and Sports Bodies eApplications." After submission, keep an eye out for further document requests by the Revenue. Make sure you submit any requested additional documents so that your application is processed.

Once your tax exemption application has been approved, you will receive a Charitable Tax exemption number (CHY). As long as you still meet the conditions that make your organization eligible for tax exemption, there is no need for a renewal application.

OBTAINING TAX EXEMPTION IN THE UNITED STATES

From the United States' perspective, foreign organizations are those that were created in countries other than the United States, its territories, or its possessions. Foreign organizations may apply for tax-exempt status on income earned in the United States in the same way that domestic organizations apply for exempt status (see Chapter 7 for details). Keep in mind that contributions by U.S. residents to foreign organizations generally are not deductible.

A foreign organization that obtains exemption as a public charity must file an information return annually (Form 990 or Form 990-EZ). A foreign organization that is a private foundation must file Form 990-PF annually. However, a foreign organization, other than a private foundation or a section 509(a)(3) supporting organization, may file Form 990-N (e-Postcard) instead of Form 990 or Form 990-EZ when its gross receipts from TIP U.S. sources are normally $50,000 or less and it has not conducted significant activity in the United States.

APPENDIX E: UNITED KINGDOM CONSIDERATIONS

CREATING ARTICLES OF INCORPORATION

When you are registering your organization in the United Kingdom, you will provide basic information about your charity including name, bank details, contact information and location, a copy of the governing document (also known as bylaws), recent accounts, and the names, contact information and birth dates of all trustees. In some cases, proof of income may be required. If so, you can provide the following:

- the scanned image of the most recent bank statement
- the PDF format of the most recent annual accounts that were published
- the scanned image of a formal funding offer endorsed by an acknowledged funding body

Be prepared to also provide this information if it is requested:

- clarity on the charitable purposes of your organization
- the operations that your organization does for the benefit of the public
- the evidence that the annual income of your organization exceeds £5,000

APPLYING FOR A REGISTRATION NUMBER

We described how you can register your charity organization in the United Kingdom. Please follow that procedure. Once your nonprofit has been registered, you will receive your registration number.

OBTAINING TAX EXEMPTION IN THE UNITED KINGDOM

As a nonprofit organization in England, you do not pay corporate tax. You can enjoy tax relief on investment income, donations, profits from trading, and when you purchase the property. On the other hand, there are times when you are expected to pay taxes, such as the payroll tax. For your nonprofit organization to be exempt from paying taxes, it should be recognized by HM Revenue and Customs (HMRC). Here are other conditions that your organization should meet for it to qualify for tax exemption:

- Its existence should be solely for the benefit of the public.
- Its main offices should be in the UK, Norway, Iceland, UE, or Liechtenstein.

It should be registered with a charity regulator, such as the Charity Commission.

OBTAINING TAX EXEMPTION IN THE UNITED STATES

From the United States' perspective, foreign organizations are those that were created in countries other than the United States, its territories, or its possessions. Foreign organizations may apply for tax-exempt status on income earned in the United States in the same way that domestic organizations apply for exempt status (see Chapter 7 for details). Keep in mind that contributions by U.S. residents to foreign organizations generally are not deductible.

A foreign organization that obtains exemption as a public charity must file an information return annually (Form 990 or Form 990-EZ). A foreign organization that is a private foundation must file Form 990-PF annually. However, a foreign organization, other than a private foundation or a section 509(a)(3) supporting organization, may file Form 990-N (e-Postcard) instead of Form 990 or Form 990-EZ when its gross receipts from TIP U.S. sources are normally $50,000 or less and it has not conducted significant activity in the United States.

REFERENCES

30 inspirational quotes for nonprofit leaders. (2023, January 2). Classy. https://www.classy.org/blog/motivational-quotes-nonprofits/

Aberdeen Group. (2016). *Definition: Visual engagement.* http://ww2. glance.net/wp-content/uploads/2016/05/ VisualEngagementROI_Aberdeen.pdf

Agency, C. R. (2017, June 22). *Income tax guide to the Non-Profit Organization (NPO) information return.* Aem. https://www.canada. ca/en/revenue-agency/services/forms-publications/publications/ t4117/income-tax-guide-non-profit-organization-information-return.html

Antonelli, A. (2017, December). *The art of forecasting contributed revenue.* Nonprofit Finance Fund. https://nff.org/blog/art-forecasting-contributed-revenue

Australian Government. (2014). *Tax basics for non-profit organizations.* https://www.ato.gov.au/uploadedfiles/content/sme/downloads/ nonprofit16966tax_basics_for_non_profit_organisations.pdf

Australian Securities and Investments Commission. (n.d.). *Registering not-for-profit or charitable organisations.* Asic.gov.au. https://asic.gov. au/for-business/registering-a-company/steps-to-register-a-company/registering-not-for-profit-or-charitable-organisations/

Australian Taxation Office. (n.d.). *Types of NFP organisations.* www.ato.-gov.au. https://www.ato.gov.au/general/aboriginal-and-torres-strait-islander-people/not-for-profit-organisations/types-of-nfp-organisations/

BoardSource. (2022, May 12). *Do we really need board committees?* BoardSource. https://boardsource.org/resources/really-need-board-committees/

Burdick, R. (n.d.). *How to claim your nonprofit profile.* Help.guidestar.org. https://help.guidestar.org/en/articles/3382584-how-to-claim-your-nonprofit-profile

Canada Revenue Agency. (2018a). *Type of corporation*. Canada.ca. https://www.canada.ca/en/revenue-agency/services/tax/busi nesses/topics/corporations/type-corporation.html

Canada Revenue Agency. (2018b, October 5). *Apply to become a registered charity*. www.canada.ca. https://www.canada.ca/en/revenue-agency/services/charities-giving/charities/registering-charitable-qualified-donee-status/apply-become-registered-charity.html

Canada Revenue Agency. (2019). *Business Registration Online – What you can do*. Canada.ca. https://www.canada.ca/en/revenue-agency/services/tax/businesses/topics/registering-your-business/busi ness-registration-online-overview.html

Charities Regulator. (n.d.). *What We Do*. https://www.charitiesregula tor.ie/en/who-we-are/what-we-do

Charity Clarity. (n.d.). *How do we rate charities?* https://www.charityclar ity.org.uk/how-do-we-rate-charities/

Charity Commissin for England and Wales. (2014). *Charitable Companies: Model Articles of Association*. https://assets.publishing. service.gov.uk/government/uploads/system/uploads/attachment_ data/file/1076196/GD1_articles_of_association_280422.pdf

Charity Navigator. (n.d.). *Ratings*. www.charitynavigator.org. https:// www.charitynavigator.org/about-us/our-methodology/ratings/? bay=content.view&cpid=32

Dominique, W. B. (2020, February 18). *Best free accounting software for nonprofits*. LoveToKnow. https://charity.lovetoknow.com/charita ble-organizations/free-accounting-software-nonprofits

Ensor, K. (2022, May 20). *Nonprofit statistics 2022: Financial, giving, and industry-based data*. Nonprofit Blog. https://donorbox.org/ nonprofit-blog/nonprofit-statistics

Farese, G. (2020). *The state of nonprofit supporters in 2020*. Resources.freewill.com. https://resources.freewill.com/the-state-of-nonprofit-supporters-in-2020

Fettke, K. (2015). *6 real estate investing success stories that will inspire you*. RealWealth. https://realwealth.com/learn/6-real-estate-investing-success-stories-that-will-inspire-you/amp/

"Fiscal Sponsorship for Nonprofits." *National Council of Nonprofits*, www.councilofnonprofits.org/running-nonprofit/administration-and-financial-management/fiscal-sponsorship-nonprofits.

Fishman, Stephen, JD. "The Pros and Cons of a Fiscal Sponsor for Nonprofits." *www.nolo.com*, Apr. 2016, www.nolo.com/legal-encyclopedia/the-pros-cons-fiscal-sponsor-nonprofits.html.

Fritz, J. (2021, July 20). *Does a nonprofit need an Employer Identification Number (EIN)?* LiveAbout. https://www.liveabout.com/what-is-an-ein-and-why-does-my-nonprofit-need-one-2501883

Funding For Good. (2022, March 13). *How many board members should a nonprofit have?* Funding for Good. https://fundingforgood.org/how-many-board-members-should-a-nonprofit-have/

GiveForms. (2022, April 20). *10 killer mission statement examples for nonprofits.* GiveForms Blog. https://www.giveforms.com/blog/10-killer-mission-statement-examples-for-nonprofits

GiveWell. (n.d.). *Our criteria for top charities.* https://www.givewell.org/how-we-work/criteria

Gov. UK. (n.d.). *Set up a charity.* https://www.gov.uk/setting-up-charity/register-your-charity?step-by-step-nav=3dd66b86-ce29-4f31-bfa2-a5a18b877f11

Government Digital Service. (2012, October 13). *Charities and tax.* Gov.UK. https://www.gov.uk/charities-and-tax/tax-reliefs

Guest Author. (2020, July 10). *Nonprofit banking: 5 things every nonprofit should know.* Nonprofit Blog. https://donorbox.org/nonprofit-blog/nonprofit-banking#6

Hamlin, A. (2020, June 12). *So you want to start a nonprofit.* https://www.aaronhamlin.com/articles/so-you-want-to-start-a-nonprofit

Hanif, B. (2022, March 18). *What are the articles of incorporation for non profit: A step-by-step guide to incorporation [with a sample template].* Glue Up. https://www.glueup.com/blog/articles-of-incorporation-for-non-profit

Harbor Compliance. (n.d.-a). *IRS Determination Letter.* https://www.harborcompliance.com/information/irs-determination-letter

Harbor Compliance. (n.d.-b). *Types of nonprofit organizations.* https://www.harborcompliance.com/information/types-of-nonprofit-organizations

Heaslip, E. (2020, March 30). *Nonprofit, not-for-profit and for-profit organizations explained*. Uschamber. https://www.uschamber.com/co/start/strategy/nonprofit-vs-not-for-profit-vs-for-profit

Henry, S. (2017). *20 Inspirational nonprofit vision statements* . Elevation Web. https://blog.elevationweb.org/nonprofit-vision-statements

Huston, H. (2020, November 6). *Filing for tax exempt status for your nonprofit*. www.wolterskluwer.com. https://www.wolterskluwer.com/en/expert-insights/filing-for-tax-exempt-status-for-your-nonprofit

Ibrisevic, I. (2021a, March 11). *How to craft your nonprofit organizational values: The complete process*. Nonprofit Blog. https://donorbox.org/nonprofit-blog/nonprofit-values

Ibrisevic, I. (2021b, June 8). *Nonprofit bylaws made easy: Tips and best practices*. Nonprofit Blog. https://donorbox.org/nonprofit-blog/nonprofit-bylaws-made-easy

IRS. (n.d.). *Employer Identification Number: Internal Revenue Service*. www.irs.gov. https://www.irs.gov/charities-non-profits/employer-identification-number

Jitasa. (12 C.E., November). *9 risk management strategies for nonprofits*. Jitasa Group. https://www.jitasagroup.com/jitasa_nonprofit_blog/risk-management-for-nonprofits/

Kapoor, S. (2022, May 17). *3 best free accounting software for nonprofits*. www.capterra.com. https://www.capterra.com/resources/top-free-accounting-software-for-nonprofit/

Kenton, W. (2019). *What everyone should know about corporations*. Investopedia. https://www.investopedia.com/terms/c/corporation.asp

Kindful. (2020, December 7). *Quickbooks for nonprofits: Your questions, answered*. Kindful. https://kindful.com/blog/quickbooks-for-nonprofits/

McKissock. (2020, December 23). *This young millionaire went from bartender to investor by age 27*. McKissock Learning. https://www.mckissock.com/blog/real-estate/success-story-flexible-jobs-melanie-bajrovic/

McRay, G. (2016, November 23). *Recordkeeping basics for nonprofits*.

Foundation Group®. https://www.501c3.org/recordkeeping-basics-for-nonprofits/

Meloni, L. (2021, August 5). *Things to look for when selecting your nonprofit board members.* Glue Up. https://www.glueup.com/blog/select-nonprofit-board

Miller, C. (2018, April 10). *Nonprofits: Six benefits to scrupulous financial records.* https://blog.concannonmiller.com/4thought/nonprofits-six-benefits-to-scrupulous-financial-records

National Council of Nonprofits. (2014a, December). *How to start a nonprofit.* https://www.councilofnonprofits.org/tools-resources/how-start-nonprofit

National Council of Nonprofits. (2014b, December 31). *Conflicts of interest.* National https://www.councilofnonprofits.org/tools-resources/conflicts-of-interest

National Council of Nonprofits. (2015, January 12). *Document retention policies for nonprofits.* fits. https://www.councilofnonprofits.org/tools-resources/document-retention-policies-nonprofits

Neo Law Group. (2016, March 6). *Starting a nonprofit: Form 1023 or Form 1023-EZ?* Nonprofit Law Blog. https://nonprofitlawblog.com/starting-a-nonprofit-form-1023-or-form-1023-ez/

Nolo. (n.d.). *How to Form a Wyoming nonprofit corporation.* https://www.nolo.com/legal-encyclopedia/forming-nonprofit-corporation-wyoming-36050.html

Nonprofit Education Survey Project. (2021). *States of COVID-19: Synthesis of state-level nonprofit reports on the impact of the COVID-19 pandemic.* Docs.google.com. https://docs.google.com/document/u/0/d/1W17H_awYEzXU26xuSOlhAZqjdR6ej_jg64p477kGIoo/mobilebasic

Nonprofit Law in England and Wales. (2013, November 24). Council on Foundations. https://cof.org/country-notes/nonprofit-law-england-waless

Nonprofit Law in Ireland. (2013, November 24). Council on Foundations. https://cof.org/country-notes/nonprofit-law-ireland

Nonprofit Leadership Center. (n.d.). *Advantages and disadvantages of starting a nonprofit organization.* https://nlctb.org/wp-content/

uploads/Advantages-and-Disadvantages-of-Starting-a-Nonprofit-Organization.pdf

NonProfitally. (n.d.). *Create Your Nonprofit Corporate Binder.* https://nonprofitally.com/start-a-nonprofit/nonprofit-corporate-binder/

NP. (2011, December 25). *Does my nonprofit need to pay tax? Understanding unrelated business income tax.* Nonprofit Quarterly. https://nonprofitquarterly.org/does-my-nonprofit-need-to-pay-tax-understanding-unrelated-business-income-tax/?gclid=CjwK CAjwo_KXBhAaEiwA2RZ8hPRHzG-w7sQ-JSyk8-ijwHiyqPx JEn7e0bpDtZ-wWPdsP130q1IpUBoCtGEQAvD_BwE

Office, A. T. (2022, March 27). *Register your NFP.* www.ato.gov.au. https://www.ato.gov.au/non-profit/getting-started/register-your-nfp/

Outsourced Acc. (2021a, January 6). *Tax exempt status for a non-profit organization.* Chartered Management Accountants. https://www.outsourcedacc.co.uk/businesscentre/tax-exempt-status-for-a-non-profit-organisation/

Peek, S. (2022, August 3). *What is a vision statement?* Business News Daily. https://www.businessnewsdaily.com/3882-vision-statement.html

PLEA. (n.d.). *Charitable activities.* https://www.plea.org/non-profit-organizations/charities/registering-as-a-charity/activities-of-the-organization

Price, N. (2018, June 4). *What are the different types of 501(c)(3) organizations?* BoardEffect. https://www.boardeffect.com/blog/what-are-the-different-types-of-501c3-organizations/

Raj. (2021, April 6). *How to start a nonprofit organization [10 step guide].* Nonprofit Blog. https://donorbox.org/nonprofit-blog/start-a-nonprofit

Reasonover, C. (2021, September 6). *50 nonprofit facts and statistics.* Foundation Group®. https://www.501c3.org/50-nonprofit-facts-and-statistics/

Replogle, M. (n.d.). *Should a nonprofit organization trademark its name or logo?* www.nolo.com. https://www.nolo.com/legal-encyclopedia/

should-a-nonprofit-organization-trademark-its-name-or-logo.html

Revenue. (n.d.). *How to apply for charitable tax exemption.* www.revenue.ie. https://www.revenue.ie/en/companies-and-charities/charities-and-sports-bodies/charitable-tax-exemption/how-to-apply-for-charitable-tax-exemption.aspx

Setting up a non-profit organization (NPO) in Ireland (n.d.). Dimitra International. https://dimitrainternational.com/en/setting-up-a-non-profit-organization-npo-in-ireland/

The Bridgespan. (n.d.). *Program evaluation.* Bridgespan.org. https://www.bridgespan.org/insights/library/nonprofit-management-tools-and-trends/program-evaluation

User, S. (n.d.). *Rating methodology.* Charity Intelligence Canada. https://www.charityintelligence.ca/charities-rating-methodology

Virginia Society of Certified Public Accountants.s. (n.d.). *Nonprofit resources.* https://www.vscpa.com/nonprofit-resources

Wellington, O. (2020, June 19). *The role and responsibilities of a nonprofit Board of Directors.* Azeus Convene. https://www.azeusconvene.com/articles/the-role-and-responsibilities-of-a-nonprofit-board-of-directors

Wingo, L. (2021, February 5). *What are the different types of nonprofits?* Https://Www.uschamber.com/Co. https://www.uschamber.com/co/start/strategy/nonprofit-designations-explained

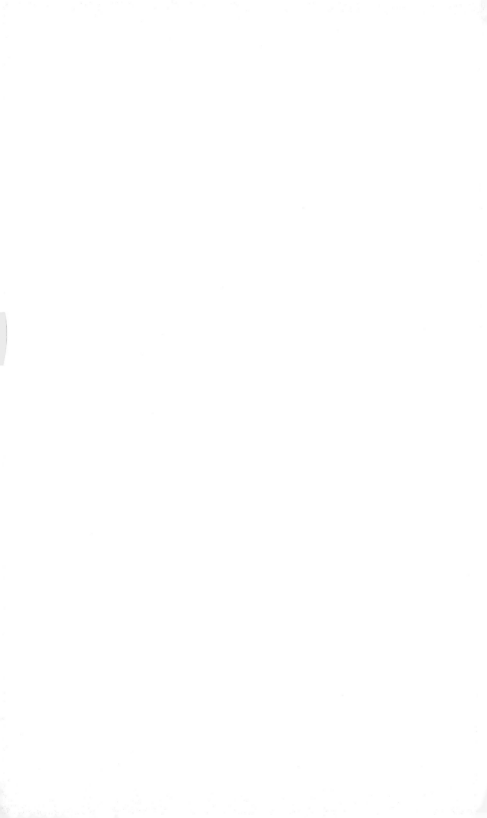

Made in the USA
Coppell, TX
29 April 2024